"As a ministry dedicated to hel[...] questions about how to deal w[...] book, P. Brian Noble offers sc[...] seeking reconciliation amid th[...]"

Jim Daly, president of Focus on the Family

"Brian Noble has provided an excellent resource in *Living Reconciled*. As you journey through this book, it will transform your thoughts and feelings so that you can live out your divine design."

Doug Clay, general superintendent of the Assemblies of God

"In *Living Reconciled*, P. Brian Noble inspires us to view our relationships with others in the context of our relationship with God. Conflict is inevitable, but reconciliation is absolutely possible when we live the gospel message. This book provides a practical foundation on which to build healthy relationships, and everyone should read it!"

Dr. Kent Mankins, pastor and licensed mental health counselor

"*Living Reconciled* feels like sitting down to coffee with a wise friend for guidance. Brian pastorally leads you on a whirlwind tour of biblical reconciliation coupled with vulnerable authenticity. This book will catalyze courageous peacemakers to live out the gospel wholeheartedly in their most difficult relationships."

Daniel Teater, president of Live at Peace Ministries

"Dealing with difficult relationships can bring out the worst in good people. But it doesn't have to be that way. Brian Noble's new book, *Living Reconciled*, offers a fresh and hopeful perspective about how to deal more effectively with challenging people. Brian's warm, conversational style and sense of humor captures the reader's attention as he demonstrates how seven courageous attitudes can bring us peace. This book is loaded with scriptural support and practical advice. As a bonus, Brian includes a thirty-one-day devotional to assist the reader in forming new healthy habits for dealing with conflict. I highly recommend *Living Reconciled* to anyone who wants to be recognized as part of God's family: 'Blessed are the peacemakers, for they will be called children of God' (Matt. 5:9)."

Laurie Stewart, vice president of Intelligent Faith

"*Living Reconciled* is a powerful call to understand gospel essentials and actually live out what Jesus has called us to do, especially when there is relational conflict. Pastor Brian speaks from the heart with gentle admonition to follow Christ and speak truth in love."

Judy Steidl, founder of Grace Mediation

"What a wonderful book! Following its principles will help Christians fulfill the mandate to glorify God. So many people live as though this life is all there is; however P. Brian Noble brings home, compellingly, the need to be mindful of the temporariness of this life. Throughout the book and the thirty-one-day devotional at the end, his 'how to' applications benefit the reader in learning to bring peace to conflicted relationships. I highly recommend *Living Reconciled*."

Oletha Barnett, founder of Conciliation Services, LLC,
professional mediator, attorney, theologian,
and conflict resolution director for Oak Cliff Bible Fellowship

"Even as a peacemaker who knows what I'm supposed to do, it's not easy for me to 'live at peace with everyone' (Rom. 12:18). So I'm grateful to Brian Noble for writing this book to help us go deeper into Scripture to see how Jesus can help us. Brian's enthusiasm for the gospel and its transforming power shines through every page. He takes familiar Bible passages and makes them come alive as he applies them to the struggle of conflict. You will be encouraged and empowered toward reconciliation by reading and applying *Living Reconciled*."

Anne Bachle Fifer, attorney, mediator,
and trainer for Peacemaker Ministries

"How did *Living Reconciled* impact me? Brian's engaging style challenged me in a current conflict to consider what it means to live as a reconciled child of God. His book reminds us that true reconciliation is based on what God has done for us through Christ. He is crazy for the gospel, and he dares his readers to be the same. I recommend *Living Reconciled*—unless you resist being crazy for the gospel."

Ted Kober, DLitt, founder/senior ambassador
of Ambassadors of Reconciliation

"Brian Noble provides indispensable biblical insight on the importance of both forgiveness and reconciliation. He systematically contrasts the distinction between living by the passions of the flesh with living in—and with—the Holy Spirit. This comparison provides profound Christian insight into how loving one's neighbor contributes to the flourishing of interpersonal relationships. With pastoral care and clarity, Noble challenges the reader to contemplate the significance of being a new creation in Christ, the indwelling of Holy Spirit in the lives of Christians, and the consequential obligation to live as a testimony to peace and reconciliation with our neighbor. In such contentious times where 'cancelation' is prized, the relevance and application of *Living Reconciled* cannot be emphasized enough."

Derryck Green, author and theologian

LIVING
RECONCILED

LIVING
RECONCILED

7 WAYS TO BRING PEACE TO YOUR
MOST DIFFICULT RELATIONSHIPS

P. BRIAN NOBLE

BakerBooks

a division of Baker Publishing Group
Grand Rapids, Michigan

Published by Baker Books
a division of Baker Publishing Group
PO Box 6287, Grand Rapids, MI 49516-6287
www.bakerbooks.com

Printed in the United States of America

Library of Congress Cataloging-in-Publication Data
Names: Noble, P. Brian, 1974– author.
Title: Living reconciled : 7 ways to bring peace to your most difficult relationships / P. Brian Noble.
Description: Grand Rapids : Baker Books, a division of Baker Publishing Group, 2022. | Includes bibliographical references.
Identifiers: LCCN 2021029311 | ISBN 9780801094309 | ISBN 9781540902023 (casebound) | ISBN 9781493434008 (ebook)
Subjects: LCSH: Interpersonal relations—Religious aspects—Christianity. | Conflict management—Religious aspects—Christianity. | Reconciliation—Religious aspects—Christianity.
Classification: LCC BV4597.52 .N63 2022 | DDC 204/.4—dc23
LC record available at https://lccn.loc.gov/2021029311

22   23   24   25   26   27   28   7   6   5   4   3   2   1

This book is dedicated to Marilyn Fargo.
Thank you for mentoring me and investing endless hours
to help me learn biblical peacemaking.

Have this attitude in yourselves which was also in Christ Jesus.

Philippians 2:5

CONTENTS

Contents

INTRODUCTION

Have you ever wanted reconciliation? Have you ever had reconciliation with someone but found it hard to maintain? I understand. I've been there. Experiencing reconciliation and maintaining it can be difficult. The more intimate the relationship, the more challenging it may seem.

Living Reconciled will help you with two things. First, you may have attempted to reconcile but the entire relationship has fallen apart, or the other person is unwilling. This book will give you seven keys to moving forward with a courageous reconciliation attitude, regardless of the other person's response. The second scenario is you have reconciled completely. However, your thoughts and feelings keep getting the best of you. *Living Reconciled* will help you transform those thoughts and feelings so that they glorify God and bring freedom in your life.

Let me tell you a story. You may have noticed that all of my writing and books are signed P. Brian Noble. I am often asked about my name. What does the *P* stand for? Because I am a pastor, people often think it means Pastor Brian Noble. However, my entire name is Paul Brian Noble. The P. doesn't stand for pastor. *P* truly is my first initial.

Growing up, I went through seasons of closeness and seasons of distance with my dad, Paul Wallace Noble. In fact, back in my hometown, about half of my friends will call me Paul while the other half will call me Brian. From first through third grade, I went by Paul. From third grade through today, I have gone by Brian. I can remember the day—I was about eight years old—that I decided I didn't want to go by my dad's name anymore. I wanted my own name. I wanted my own identity.

My dad is very blunt, and I struggled to understand him. I misunderstood a lot of his actions and parenting techniques and his personality. Not too long after I made that decision to change my name I entered my teen years, which were no doubt fraught with name-calling from my peers, tension at home, and all the stuff that goes with being a young man. It was a rough set of years relationally.

Then, at age twenty-one, I was challenged by God to be completely reconciled with my dad. God encouraged me to let go of the past and have a new outlook and view of my dad. I had come to know Jesus through repentance and had been baptized; I knew I needed a Jesus reconciliation. Long story short, my dad and I reconciled. As a symbol of this reconciliation, I decided to put the P. back on my name. Every day when I sign my name, I am reminded I am reconciled. I love my dad and my mom and my stepdad and my stepmom so much. They are all amazing people.

This book is a journey about reconciliation: what that means from a God-perspective and how to find reconciliation in your life. Throughout this book, we are going to use one chapter of Scripture as the roadmap for this journey, 2 Corinthians 5. Let's read through it together as we begin:

> For we know that if the earthly tent which is our house is torn down, we have a building from God, a house not made with hands, eternal in the heavens. For indeed in this house we groan, longing to be clothed with our dwelling from heaven, inasmuch as we, having put it on, will not be found naked. For indeed while we are in this tent, we groan, being burdened, because we do not want to be unclothed but to be clothed, so that what is mortal will be swallowed up by life. Now He who prepared us for this very purpose is God, who gave to us the Spirit as a pledge.

Therefore, being always of good courage, and knowing that while we are at home in the body we are absent from the Lord—for we walk by faith, not by sight—we are of good courage, I say, and prefer rather to be absent from the body and to be at home with the Lord. Therefore we also have as our ambition, whether at home or absent, to be pleasing to Him. For we must all appear before the judgment seat of Christ, so that each one may be recompensed for his deeds in the body, according to what he has done, whether good or bad.

Therefore, knowing the fear of the Lord, we persuade men, but we are made manifest to God; and I hope that we are made manifest also in your consciences. We are not again commending ourselves to you but are giving you an occasion to be proud of us, so that you will have an answer for those who take pride in appearance and not in heart. For if we are beside ourselves, it is for God; if we are of sound mind, it is for you. For the love of Christ controls us, having concluded this, that one died for all, therefore all died; and He died for all, so that they who live might no longer live for themselves, but for Him who died and rose again on their behalf.

Therefore from now on we recognize no one according to the flesh; even though we have known Christ according to the flesh, yet now we know Him in this way no longer. Therefore if anyone is in Christ, he is a new creature; the old things passed away; behold, new things have come. Now all these things are from God, who reconciled us to Himself through Christ and gave us the ministry of reconciliation, namely, that God was in Christ reconciling the world to Himself, not counting their trespasses against them, and He has committed to us the word of reconciliation.

Therefore, we are ambassadors for Christ, as though God were making an appeal through us; we beg you on behalf of Christ, be reconciled to God. He made Him who knew no sin to be sin on our behalf, so that we might become the righteousness of God in Him.

I encourage you to read this out loud. Underline parts that jump out or intrigue you. Highlight parts you have questions about. Circle words or phrases that repeat. This Scripture passage clearly shows us seven courageous attitudes to reconciliation. They can change us, transform us, and make us more and more like the Savior we serve.

This will be a journey—a fun journey. It is a journey that I am on. It is how I change my thinking about my circumstances and the conflicts I experience on a daily basis. Even while writing this book, I kept thinking about how I need to apply *this* reconciliation attitude or *that* one to an area of my life or to a relationship with a specific person. Guess what? When I stopped and applied it, my heart changed.

My hope is, as we journey together, God's Word will transform you like it is transforming me, and you will experience God's grace and peace and reconciliation, even in your toughest relationships.

1

Be Real

Tough Relationships Are Inevitable

What do I really know about this world? I don't understand this life. How often have you thought that? Don't deny it happens. We all have thoughts like that sometimes. In fact, chances are high you are probably like me and think this world is a very confusing place to live. We can go from having the best day ever to the worst day ever in a matter of moments.

In 1999, my wife (Tanya) and I were pregnant with our first child. Well, Tanya was. But we were both so excited about our child's arrival. Tanya's plan was to have a completely natural birth. Now, if it were me, I would not choose "natural" in pretty much anything medical; natural just seems so painful. I'd read about the fall and the curse in Genesis 3. Scripture is crystal clear: God told Eve, "I will greatly multiply your pain in childbirth," and if that were not enough, God continued on to explain that "in pain you will bring forth children" (v. 16). So the natural conclusion I came to is that labor was going to hurt. However, as a supportive husband, I decided to respect Tanya's desire to go through this thing "naturally."

The day finally came that Tanya began her labor pains. Our home was about fifty minutes away from Holy Family Hospital. The distance made us nervous, so we rushed to the hospital. Ran in! And to our disappointment, it was not quite time yet. Tanya needed to progress more before the hospital would admit her. I suggested we walk around a local mall for a few hours, and then maybe she would be ready. By the way—attention all husbands—if your wife is in labor, walking around a mall, or any public place, is a bad idea. Write it down. Get a tattoo! Walking around a mall while your wife is expecting: bad idea. Talking to friends in the mall while your wife is in labor is also a bad idea. Wanting to buy fast food at the mall while your wife is in labor: a very bad idea.

Despite the pain and my less-than-stellar suggestion, our excitement grew and grew. Finally, we went back to the hospital; surely it had to be time. Nope! We reluctantly went back home. Eventually, however, we were back at Holy Family Hospital and Tanya was admitted. This is where things went from best day ever to worst day ever and back to best day ever.

Best day ever: we were in the process of having our first baby. Pain and all, we were thrilled.

Then the nurses started fussing. One nurse came into the room. She left. Another nurse came in with the first nurse. They explained that the baby's heart rate was dropping, and they were very concerned for both mom and baby. They had Tanya get into different positions. Nothing seemed to help. The heart rate just kept falling.

Worst day ever: the next thing I knew, they were telling us they needed to do an emergency caesarean section.

My heart started to race, and Tanya expressed her disappointment over not having a natural birth. But in a matter of moments, they had Tanya out of the room we were in, and I was standing in another little room putting on scrubs. I was praying and praying, "Lord, please don't take my wife home. Please help my baby be born alive."

"Paul?" said a nurse. "Paul Noble!"

Oh, the nurse was talking to me; I wasn't used to being called by my first name.

"Are you —?"

I quickly replied, "Yes, I am Paul Brian Noble."

"Come with me," said the nurse.

The nurse took me into an operating room. My wife was lying on a bed, not moving. Fear rushed through my body. "Have a seat on this stool," said the nurse. Then Tanya looked at me. She was afraid. She was disappointed. The look in her eyes was *Today is the worst day ever*. She wanted a natural birth.

The doctor came in, explained a few things, and then began. In only a few moments—painful ones for Tanya (we found out later that the medicine they gave her didn't work on her)—the C-section was done.

Best day ever: suddenly, I was holding my brand-new baby boy. He was perfect. He had a little cut on his head from the surgery, but besides that, he was perfect.

~~~

Childbirth is an apt description of the reconciliation process. Just as a birth can go from smooth to bumpy and back, so can reconciliation. At one point, you might be rejoicing: "We made it through our conflict!" But one little misplaced, misunderstood word can rub one party or the other the wrong way, and you find yourself five steps back. This is not unusual. There is still hope. Or you want to reconcile, and the other person won't try. Then the other person wants to reconcile, and you won't try. Reconciliation can be frustrating. Yet at the same time, it can be exciting.

However, we live in a temporal and fallen world. And it is not going to get better. In fact, it is actually getting worse. This very fact of our current state is critical to reconciliation. I know this reality check sounds ultra-depressing, but there are four realities we all must face:

1. We are all going to die.
2. We are all going to groan.

3. We are all afraid of being naked.
4. We are all going to be burdened.

You're probably reading this book because you have a relationship that is strained, tense, or filled with conflict. Below, we will use 2 Corinthians 5 to look at these four realities through a temporal lens. (In the next chapter, we will go back through the same Bible verses and look at them through an eternal lens.) So get ready to be depressed. Get ready to want to give up. But if you will hang with me, you will begin to grasp the amazing journey we are on. A journey of hope. A journey of becoming a reconciler and living in reconciliation.

You Are Going to Die: Your Tent Is Temporary

> For we know that if the earthly tent which is our house is torn down, we have a building from God, a house not made with hands, eternal in the heavens. (2 Cor. 5:1)

Look at this verse closely. Remember that Scripture has the power to change lives. Scripture is a living word, filled with hope. It is a source of comfort.

Let's start by focusing on the first half of this verse: "For we know that if the earthly tent which is our house is torn down." So many in our current world do not want to admit this truth: we are all going to die. But I do, and I will try to be as clear as possible. We—you and I—live in earthly tents, which are temporary structures, not meant to last. Not only that, but your tent is going to be torn down. You are going to die!

"Okay, hold on," you may protest. "You are writing a book to bring me hope and comfort, and the first thing you tell me is I live in a tent that will be torn down, and I'm going to die? Done! I'm not reading any more."

Wait. Please keep reading. This point is critical. If you get this one thing wrong, the entire rest of your life is going to be way more difficult. Okay, that may be a slight exaggeration; however,

I truly believe that if you think this earth and this life are meant to be perfect, then you are going to be a very depressed person.

How is that thought comforting? Well, if you are connecting with your inner Aladdin, singing "A Whole New World," you will someday wake up and realize that if *this* is the new world, the fantastic point of view, and the dream, then something must be wrong with you—because this world is disappointing, disillusioning, and depressing. This earth is filled with tents that will be torn down. This is not a new world; it is a fallen world. It is not a fantastic point of view; it is a temporary point of view.

My family loved to go camping when I was growing up. Mom and Tom, my stepdad, slept in a camping trailer, and we kids slept in a tent. (Although my sister somehow always ended up in the trailer.) We always arrived at the campground late the first night, because we couldn't leave until Mom and Tom got off of work, then we would have to drive a few hours to get to where we were camping.

My brother and I would set up the tent in the dark. First, we would try to find a level place. Second, we would try to make sure there were no roots, rocks, or pinecones that might cause a person discomfort and lost sleep. Third, we would put the tent together. Fourth, we would place our sleeping bags, pillows, and anything else we felt we would need to be comfortable inside the tent. Fifth, we would try not to think about the grizzly bears that could rip through the tent and eat us. Sixth, we would try to fall asleep fast, thinking happy thoughts.

My brother would always fall asleep quickly, but I would lie there, wide awake, noticing the rock, the root, the pinecone we'd somehow missed, and how dark it was outside. I'd start to hear sounds I hadn't noticed before: the running brook, the owl, the wolves howling. My perfect spot would become not so perfect. My tent—my barrier from the outside—seemed thin, unsafe, and insufficient to protect me.

Nine out of ten times, it would start to rain. Then I would wonder if the tent was waterproof. Then the wind would start to blow, and I'd start to think about the trees around us falling on the tent. Eventually, I would fall asleep. And in what seemed like only a moment, a bright light came shining on the tent: hot, muggy, so uncomfortable. It was morning. And my first morning thought was, *I hate tents.*

Here is my point: tents are not comfortable. Tents are temporary. Tents are not that safe. Tents are insignificant to protect us from the world around us. Paul says that our bodies—our tents—are our houses. Our tents are frail. Our tents hold our emotions, our thoughts, our desires, our personalities, our likes, our dislikes, our fears, and our lives—who we are as individuals.

I would rather Paul had said, "For we know that if this earthly bomb shelter which is our house . . ." At least a bomb shelter would be strong, mighty, and able to withstand anything thrown at it. Drop a nuclear bomb on a shelter, and it will be just fine. Send a storm? No problem. Throw in some relational tension? Not a big deal. But unfortunately, Paul said *tent*. (For all of you out there feeling the need to point out Paul would have not known what a bomb shelter was, I get it. I know, and thanks for your input.)

And here's the thing. Paul doesn't only say we have a tent; he also points out that the tent is torn down. That is even worse. What we do have is flimsy and will be destroyed someday. Now that is depressing.

What does your life, housed in this tent-like body, have to do with reconciliation? What connection does it have with how you interact with God and with others? What does it matter? I will give you a hint. When the winds of life come and force your flimsy, temporary tent to interact with my flimsy, temporary tent, it becomes messy very fast. But wait! It gets worse. Let's look at the next verse.

You Are Going to Groan: Your Soul Is Uncomfortable

For indeed in this house we groan, longing to be clothed with our dwelling from heaven. (2 Cor. 5:2)

The insides of humanity have been groaning since sin entered into the world. We have been squeezed by our circumstances. We have been pressed by trials. A tent does not do much to push back on circumstances or trials. We sigh. We are in distress.

One of my favorite psalms is Psalm 42, included below with emphasis on the groaning I see the psalmist talking about. I am not including this psalm to depress you; I am using it to illustrate how people throughout history have been groaning. They have been calling out to God. They have felt as you feel.

Psalm 42

As the deer pants for the water brooks,
So *my soul pants* for You, O God.
My soul thirsts for God, for the living God;
When shall I come and appear before God?
My tears have been my food day and night,
While they say to me all day long, "Where is your God?"
These things I remember and I *pour out my soul within me*.
For I used to go along with the throng and lead them in
    procession to the house of God,
With the voice of joy and thanksgiving, a multitude
    keeping festival.

Why are you in despair, O my soul?
And why have you become *disturbed within me*?
Hope in God, for I shall again praise Him
For the help of His presence.
O my God, my soul is in *despair within me*;
Therefore I remember You from the land of the Jordan
And the peaks of Hermon, from Mount Mizar.
Deep calls to deep at the sound of Your waterfalls;
All Your breakers and Your *waves have rolled over me*.
The Lord will command His lovingkindness in the
    daytime;
And His song will be with me in the night,
A prayer to the God of my life.

I will say to God my rock, "*Why have You forgotten me*?
Why do I go mourning because of the oppression of the
    enemy?"
As a *shattering of my bones*, my adversaries revile me,
While they say to me all day long, "Where is your God?"
Why are you in despair, O my soul?

And why have you become disturbed within me?
Hope in God, for I shall yet praise Him,
The help of my countenance and my God.

This is the type of groaning our souls can have for reconciliation with God and with others. I don't know about you, but if I am being completely transparent, between the trials of being raised in a divorced family, the trials of marriage, the trials of raising kids, and the trials of providing for my family, I have experienced every one of these groanings.

However, there is light at the end of this psalm. Did you know that some believe Psalm 42 is linked to Psalm 43 and might actually be one poem? With that perspective in mind, read on.

Psalm 43

Vindicate me, O God, and plead my case against an
    ungodly nation;
O deliver me from the deceitful and unjust man!
For You are the God of my strength; why have You
    rejected me?
Why do I go mourning because of the oppression of the
    enemy?

O send out Your light and Your truth, let them lead me;
Let them bring me to Your holy hill
And to Your dwelling places.
Then I will go to the altar of God,
To God my exceeding joy;
And upon the lyre I shall praise You, O God, my God.

Why are you in despair, O my soul?
And why are you disturbed within me?
Hope in God, for I shall again praise Him,
The help of my countenance and my God.

Today you may be groaning. Yet I believe God is going to help your countenance as you interact with his Scripture. However, I don't want to get ahead of myself, so let's go to the next verse.

You Are Fearful of Being Exposed

Inasmuch as we, having put it on, will not be found naked. (2 Cor. 5:3)

Just a reminder, "it" in this verse refers to our heavenly covering. So as you read this passage, you may be thinking, *The Scripture is actually saying NOT be found naked.* This is true, and we will look at that in the next chapter. However, I want to uncover a common fear we all have of being exposed. Remember, in this chapter I'm setting up the current state we live in—the fallen state, the sinful state. Understanding where we are is so critical to living in reconciliation.

I can remember having a recurring dream as a kid. In this dream, I would wake up and be late for school. I would rush out of the house. I would get on the bus, and all the kids would be laughing. I couldn't figure it out. Then I would show up at school and look down—and feel humiliated because I was wearing only my underwear. I would run to the bathroom and try to hide. It was the most devastating dream. You probably had the same dream or something similar. Or maybe you didn't, but I am going to tell myself you did because it makes me feel better about myself.

The world we live in makes us feel incredibly exposed. We have a desire not to be found naked, not to be found vulnerable. This is why so many people can fight all the way to church and yet put a smile on when they show up at the front door. Is it that we are all hypocrites? No—or maybe. It is simply that we can all silo, or separate ourselves off from other believers around us. We don't want to be exposed. We live in a world that desires authenticity and then places only the highlights on social media. We never want to be seen as less than. Not enough. Naked!

The cover-up has been happening from the beginning. As human beings, we have always tried to shield ourselves—to show that we can, on our own, handle life and all that is thrown at us. This is why people wait until they are one to two years into a conflict, on average, before calling Peacemaker Ministries (of which I am CEO). They want to be reconciled and want the relationship to be made right, but for years they have not glorified God and have sinned against each other. Often, they then ask us to reconcile their differences in a few hours. Quick reconciliation is possible with Jesus, but not practical with humans.

Why do we have this fear of being exposed? Let's go back to the beginning of humankind and look at a few Scriptures about Adam and Eve.

> And the man and his wife were *both naked and were not ashamed*. (Gen. 2:25)

> Then the eyes of both of them were opened, and *they knew that they were naked*; and they sewed fig leaves together and made themselves loin *coverings*. They heard the sound of the LORD God walking in the garden in the cool of the day, and the man and his wife *hid themselves from the presence of the LORD God* among the trees of the garden. Then the LORD God called to the man, and said to him, "Where are you?" He said, "I heard the sound of You in the garden, and *I was afraid because I was naked; so I hid myself*." And He said, "Who told you that you were naked? Have you eaten from the tree of which I commanded you not to eat?" (3:7–11)

What happened between Genesis 2:25 and 3:7–11? Genesis 3:1–6 happened: deception, disobedience, and sin. Sin is the reason we are so afraid to be exposed. Sin is the reason we are going to die, sin is the reason we groan, and sin is the reason we long to be clothed.

> When the woman saw that the tree was good for food, and that it was a delight to the eyes, and that the tree was desirable to make one wise, she took from its fruit and ate; and she gave also to her husband with her, and he ate. (v. 6)

How does sin play out in our relationships? How does sin play into our reconciliation? We are exposed. We are found unclothed. Naked. So, we hide. We avoid God's presence. God is calling out through the Holy Spirit, "Where are you?" And as humans, we have clothed ourselves in self-righteousness and are hiding. But when we try to clothe ourselves with anything less than Jesus Christ and him crucified, it ultimately ends in nothing more than fig leaves.

You Are Burdened

> For indeed while we are in this tent, we groan, being burdened, because we do not want to be unclothed but to be clothed, so that what is mortal will be swallowed up by life. (2 Cor. 5:4)

Being burdened! Think through this. The tent is thin. The tent is flimsy. The tent does not protect, redeem, or save. The tent not only affects each of us personally but every relationship we have, including our relationship with God. I am convinced that if we do not accurately understand life in this fallen world, we will not quickly reconcile with God and with those around us. We'll be lost in the weeds.

Weeds are normal, and produce is a miracle. Let me show you what I mean.

Since the Great Depression, my family has had a fifty-acre farm in the Yakima Valley of central Washington. We have vineyards, cattle, pastures, and a couple of different gardens. I can remember each spring we would go out and rototill the ground. As a kid, I can remember thinking, *Wow, that looks so good.* The soil was rich, and it looked so nice newly turned and ready to use. Then we would plant rows of corn, watermelons, onions, potatoes, tomatoes, squash, and many other fruits and vegetables. We used a gravity irrigation system that worked well because we were on a hill.

Do you know what else we had to do to get a great amount of produce out of all that planting? We had to weed. Weeds are normal and should be expected in a garden of any size. What if my family had lived as if weeds were not normal? What if we had told each other, "Oh, don't worry; weeds won't come. Weeds won't grow"?

I can pretend, I can hope, I can have faith, and I can believe, but weeds will come. We would spend days weeding our gardens.

I felt at the time like I did a lot of the work, but looking back, I see my dad did most of it. Why the burden of having to weed? If life were fair, we wouldn't have to. Well, the answer is simple: we live in a fallen world. Weeds are normal. The very fact that anything grows in this fallen world is a miracle—an act of God.

Go back to 2 Corinthians 5:4 and read it again. We are burdened because we do not want to be unclothed. We do not want to be exposed. To be *burdened* means to be weighed down, loaded up, heavy, or oppressed. Let the Word of God wash over you. You are burdened because of the fear of being exposed, the fear of being found in your sin, the fear of dying.

LIVING RECONCILED

We'll add to this list each chapter. Here is our first practical discovery that will help you maintain reconciliation:

1. Conflict is inevitable, for we live in a fallen world.

REVIEW AND RECAP

- We are all going to die.
- We are all going to experience difficulties.
- We are all afraid of being vulnerable and insufficient.
- We are all going to be weighed down by trouble.

Jesus answered, "The foremost is, 'Hear, O Israel! The Lord our God is one Lord; and you shall love the Lord your God with all your heart, and with all your soul, and with all your mind, and with all your strength.' The second is this, 'You shall love your neighbor as yourself.' There is no other commandment greater than these." (Mark 12:29–31)

How is living in a temporal world affecting your relationship with God?

How is living in a temporal world affecting your relationship with others?

Which part of your tent, your fallenness, is causing a God-honoring relationship to be difficult?

What are you relationally groaning about?

What has been a burden to you?

What makes you afraid of being exposed?

2

≈

Be Brave

Reconciliation Is Eventual

Have you ever thought about how awesome heaven will be? There are many songs, books, and sermons about the splendor of heaven. I do not know how accurate most of those speculations are; however, I do know we will not be disappointed, and heaven will be worth the journey to get there. What excites me more than the streets and the structures of heaven is the reconciled relationship we will have with God and with each other. We will have more days whole and complete with God than we will ever have in this fallen world.

> And I heard a loud voice from the throne, saying, "Behold, the tabernacle of God is among men, and He will dwell among them, and they shall be His people, and God Himself will be among them, and He will wipe away every tear from their eyes; and there will no longer be any death; there will no longer be any mourning, or crying, or pain; the first things have passed away." (Rev. 21:3–4)

In my work through Peacemaker Ministries, I have encountered some people who say they can't be reconciled, while others say they do not want to be reconciled. Still others say they want to be reconciled, but their words and actions are everything counterproductive to reconciliation—and yet the fact is, heaven will be filled with reconciled people. Some want an easy life now, so they are selfish, fail to be fully engaged at work, or murder people with the anger of their heart—seeking a happiness now that they will never find.

You see, *now* is the time to stand on the Word of God. Heaven is the time for happiness and ease for all believers. Yes, *all* believers in Jesus—all who have repented of their sin; turned to God; and placed their hope in the death, burial, resurrection, and appearance of Jesus Christ (1 Cor. 15:1–8)—will be in heaven, *even the ones you are not reconciled with.* I don't want to go far down this road, but if you are unwilling to reconcile with someone else, I would strongly encourage you to read Jesus's view of this in Matthew 18:21–35.

But for our purposes here, let's look at 2 Corinthians 5:1–4 again and see what Paul has to say about eternity. Get ready. Get excited! God is good, and we are on a great journey together.

A Building from God

> For we know that if the earthly tent which is our house is torn down, we have a *building from God*, a house not made with hands, eternal in the heavens. (2 Cor. 5:1)

When we die, we have a building from God. Notice the contrast. We go from a flimsy, temporary tent to a strong, everlasting building. This is amazing! God's buildings are permanent. God's buildings are sturdy, firm, quality.

Jesus is the foundation for God's buildings. "For no man can lay a foundation other than the one which is laid, which is Jesus Christ" (1 Cor. 3:11). This is so critical. There is no other foundation than Jesus Christ. When I am in conflict or tension, I think of the words of Edward Mote's hymn, "My Hope Is Built on Nothing Less."

> My hope is built on nothing less
> Than Jesus' blood and righteousness.
> I dare not trust the sweetest frame
> But wholly lean on Jesus' name[1]

This song has meant so much to me, and it continues to remind me that reconciliation is eventual. In March 2017, Isabella, my daughter who was born with Rett Syndrome (a genetic disorder that causes her not to be able to walk or talk), had surgery to fix her scoliosis, but the surgery went very wrong. When they straightened her back, Isabella lost her ability to swallow. She was drowning in her own saliva. I was leaning over her bed in the pediatric intensive care unit at our local hospital. It had been a long week. She was on a vent, and we were trying to decide what to do. My eyes were looking at her tent, her physical body, but my heart was peeking into heaven, singing, "My hope is built on nothing less." One day Isabella's body will be fully reconciled by Jesus's blood, and she will stand before his throne 100 percent whole.

The foundation of Jesus is the only foundation in heaven. There is no sinking sand in heaven. There is no other rock than Jesus. His blood and righteousness will be fully realized by those who believe in him. We will be able to stand faultless before the throne of God only because of Jesus. And guess what? We will each be reconciled to God! And we will each be reconciled to all others.

We are made by God, aren't we? Yes. But what happens in our earthly bodies, both physically and spiritually, shapes us. Every time we get sick, every time we fall down, every time we choose what food to eat shapes our human bodies—for good or ill. And every time we argue, grumble, worship, and love, we are also shaping our human bodies. Thus, our earthly bodies are being formed by human hands too. But in heaven, our souls will finally find rest. Why? Our new building will not be made with human hands but by God alone. Our new body will be eternal and not temporal. Look at how this verse reads in the New Living Translation of the Bible.

> For we know that when this earthly tent we live in is taken down (that is, when we die and leave this earthly body), we will have a house in heaven, an eternal body made for us by God himself and not by human hands. (v. 1 NLT)

When this verse talks about our body, it is talking about the entire part of us that makes us human. The physical body and the soul. Yes, it is talking about the externals as well as the internals of our humanness.

The thought of my physical body being made completely brand-new is exciting. I don't know about you, but I have certain things that just hurt, ache, and do not work very well. Every morning when I wake up, it seems like something else hurts. I know, I know, many of you are thinking, *How old is this guy? Isn't he only forty-five? Just wait until you are seventy, eighty, or ninety, pal*. I can't imagine. All I know is I should probably purchase stock in Advil.

The idea of having a new physical body is exciting, but even more intriguing than that is my new internal humanness. We will have brand-new emotions. Many of us have been wounded by our past. People have hurt us, and we have hurt people. The context of our pain will be completely redeemed, and a new context will come. It will be an exciting day when our feelings are aligned 100 percent with God. We will be free to place our hope in God. Hope will be fulfilled and evident right before our eyes.

We will have brand-new thinking, praise God! Let me say it again, louder: PRAISE GOD! If you are like me, sometimes your past consumes too much of your present thinking. It is easy to get stinking thinking. The triggers of past hurts can flow into our minds, but in heaven, all the triggers will be gone. The smells that used to generate horrible thoughts will be brand-new. I can't wait. Our bodies will be eternal, including our thinking.

We will have brand-new desires too. Can you imagine having 100 percent holy desires? It is almost beyond our understanding; however, in heaven, our desires, cravings, and appetites will be satisfied as we taste and see that the Lord is good.

We will also have redeemed personalities. My personality gets in my way all the time. In heaven, our unfallen personalities, our true personalities, our God-given personalities will come out. Oh, how sweet it will be to live in our eternal bodies. My personality, my uniqueness, will not irritate others. The unique things about others will not irritate me. I don't know how this will work exactly, but I do know it will work in heaven. It will work in the absence of sin. It will work in our eternal bodies.

We will have redeemed perceptions. The way we sense things will be 100 percent accurate and redeemed. Our worldview will be adjusted to God's worldview. I will no longer be able to simply excuse away my sometimes-errant views by saying, "Well, that is my perception." It won't be my perception anymore—I will be seeing through God's lens.

Longing to Be Clothed

> For indeed in this house we groan, *longing to be clothed* with our dwelling from heaven. (2 Cor. 5:2)

What is the greatest longing you have in your life? If you are like me, I bet you can't wait until your tent turns into clothing from heaven and 100 percent of your fallenness is taken away. Think about the difference that will make in our relationships. The NLT states 2 Corinthians 5:2 this way: "We grow weary in our present bodies, and we long to put on our heavenly bodies like new clothing."

There is a saying: "They are so heavenly minded they are no earthly good." I just haven't found that to be true. I find in myself—and most Christians—that often I am so earthly minded I am not any heavenly good. Let's set our minds on heaven. Let's take a moment to earnestly consider what it means to desire or long for heaven.

If you are longing for a place of peace, heaven is that place. Jesus is the Prince of Peace (Isa. 9:6; Eph. 2:14). In heaven, we will get to live with and be ruled by him. We groan on earth simply because we have an absence of peace. But what exactly is peace? *Peace* is an interesting word, because while most of us know when we don't have it, we struggle to describe peace when we have it. Here is what I know about peace: when Tanya and I are at peace, I know it, and when we are not at peace, I also know it.

The Lord is peace. In the Old Testament, he is called *Yahweh-shalom* (Judg. 6:24) or the Prince of Peace (Isa. 9:6). God is also referred to as the King of Peace (Heb. 7:2). God is ultimate peace. Yet peace is not his only characteristic, and none of his characteristics contradict each other. While I don't know how that works, exactly, I do know it does work. This is important, because as we long for heaven, we have to accept the fact that God is the King, the Messiah, the Prince of Peace. His kingdom is filled with peace. Hallelujah! To live experiencing God's peace will be fabulous.

Heaven is a safe place.[2] The longing to be clothed with safety is real. We live in a fallen world that struggles to experience safety in our communities, our relationships, and our families. In Scripture, we have a guarantee heaven will be a place of safety. That is what we all want for every relationship we have: a safe place.

Heaven is a war zone–free place.[3] Wars are all around us; some wars are nation against nation, some are religious, some are spiritual, some are relational, and some are internal. The enemy of our souls knows that if he can divide humanity, he can keep us from serving Jesus Christ. That is why every war ultimately is a spiritual war (Eph. 6:12). The war you are in probably has some relational elements, but ultimately it is a spiritual struggle. Knowing the battlefields we live in, doesn't heaven sound like a great place? The King of Peace will rule all, and we will no longer have wars. Yet this doesn't mean we can't experience God's peace now, while we're in the midst of spiritual or physical earthly war. As believers, we always have God's peace with us, in us, around us, and before us.

Heaven is an anxiety-free place. Have you ever had anxiety hit you like a ton of bricks? It is horrible! It can be debilitating. In heaven there will be no more anxiety nor any uneasiness, nervousness, or uncertain outcomes. Won't that be exciting? We will be clothed with peace. The disruption and despair of our souls will give way to perfect rest.

Heaven is a place of provision. There will be great living quarters in heaven (John 14:3) and amazing banquets (Rev. 7:16–17). As believers in Jesus, we will have more days celebrating in the presence of God in right relationship with him and with other believers than we will ever have on this earth. I long to be clothed with the provision that only heaven can bring.

Here are some more descriptions of God's kingdom, which all of us who are his children will someday enjoy:

- Heaven is a place of rest.
- Heaven is a place of justice.
- Heaven is a place of fullness.
- Heaven is a place of worship.
- Heaven is a place of reconciliation.
- Heaven is a place of love.
- Heaven is a place of freedom.
- Heaven is a place of comfort.

And there is so much more to heaven beyond anything we can even comprehend. All I know is heaven's clothing is going to be amazing. Do your heart and soul and body groan for this fabulous clothing? I want you to be encouraged with the knowledge that you are not at your final destination yet. Heaven is a much better place.

Not Found Naked

> Inasmuch as we, having put it on, *will not be found naked*. (2 Cor. 5:3)

Whenever I see an interesting verse like 2 Corinthians 5:3, I like to read it in several translations.

- If indeed by putting it on we may not be found naked (ESV).
- If so be that being clothed we shall not be found naked (KJV).
- So that by putting it on we may not be found naked (RSV).
- After we have put it on, we won't be naked (GW).
- Because when we are clothed, we will not be found naked (NIV).
- For we will put on heavenly bodies; we will not be spirits without bodies (NLT).

Look at what is repeated over and over in each translation: in heaven, we will not be found naked or be a spirit without a body. The beginning of each translation is slightly different, but the end or the thrust of the verse is the same: heaven is a great place, and we will not be found naked there.

In heaven, we truly get a new body that is clothed. It seems to me that everything in this world tries to expose or reveal personal things—not for the purpose of providing healing or forgiveness but to bring down people in mockery and shame. I love the fact that in heaven's eternal perspective, my sin is completely and 100 percent dealt with, paid for, and removed. And in heaven I will finish being completely transformed—not running around naked and embarrassed about my sin.

I like to say that the devil exposes and Jesus covers.

> And when [Jesus] came out onto the land [of the Gerasenes], He was met by a man from the city who was possessed with demons; and who had not put on any clothing for a long time, and was not living in a house, but in the tombs. Seeing Jesus, he cried out and fell before Him, and said in a loud voice, "What business do we have with each other, Jesus, Son of the Most High God? I beg You, do not torment me." (Luke 8:27–28)

We do not know if the demons convinced the man to run around naked or the man was a nudist, but we do know that he "had not put on any clothing for a long time," and he was demon-possessed. The devil wants to expose our nakedness, our weakness, our sins, and our faults—not for any redemptive purpose but to simply embarrass us and make us vulnerable. The devil exposes, accuses, kills, steals, and destroys. But Jesus covers, pays, gives, and comforts. When the Gerasenes came to see what had happened, they "found the man from whom the demons had gone out, sitting down at the feet of Jesus, clothed and in his right mind" (v. 35).

We are in a world of taking off and putting on. While in the final day we will be clothed completely with Jesus, let's look together at what Christ tells us to take off and put on right now. First, the Word calls us to take off the "deeds of darkness and put on the armor of light" (Rom. 13:12). This change should definitely be seen in our relationships. It is always amazing to me how immature I can be in some of my most intimate relationships. I find it too easy with my wife to default back to those things I have taken off—like strife, jealousy, anger, and annoyance. God desires that we be clothed with his light. He desires that both now and in heaven we be completely filled with compassion, kindness, joy, and so much more.

Second, we are challenged to put on the new self (Eph. 4:20–24), the self that in heaven will be completely put on, never to be removed. This new self is created in the likeness of God, in righteousness, holiness, and truth just as Jesus is "full of grace and truth" (John 1:14). When we put on the new self, we are full of, or have the opportunity to be full of, grace and truth. In our relationships, we can balance the elements but ultimately understand that it is only because of "grace upon grace" that we can interact (John 1:16).

You and I are both full of grace and truth. Why? Because of Jesus inside us, the new self on each of us, and the power of the Holy Spirit. I don't feel very full of grace at times, but it doesn't matter how I feel. What matters is who Jesus is. The new self we are putting on is being renewed to a true understanding (Col. 3:10).

Third, we are to "put on a heart of compassion, kindness, gentleness, humility, and patience" (v. 12). These are attributes of the new self I tend to take off. I remove kindness. I throw gentleness in the dirty laundry hamper. I take my will-powered patience off like a smelly sock. Why would I do this? Because these attributes, these acts of the new self, are from Jesus and must be empowered by Jesus; we cannot clothe ourselves in our own strength.

These attributes give us a picture of heaven. Heaven is a place of compassion, kindness, gentleness, humility, patience, and so much more. Inasmuch as we put on our heavenly clothing now, we find ourselves less naked. Yet I know in relationship after relationship it is so easy to remove these things. Here is the bottom line: don't be naked. Jesus is available today, and he can set us free. We can live and interact in the newness of life he provides, now in part and fully in heaven, where we will be completely, newly clothed for eternity.

Swallowed Up by Life

> For indeed while we are in this tent, we groan, being burdened, because we do not want to be unclothed but to be clothed, so that *what is mortal will be swallowed up by life.* (2 Cor. 5:4)

The imagery of being swallowed up is powerful. I am sitting in a coffee shop right now, thinking, *How do I explain this? How do I connect with this imagery and truth?* Then it hits me. That which is coffee is swallowed up by me. Others no longer see the coffee I have consumed—they see just me, a happy man.

Our fallen humanness is our mortality. Our tent is our mortality. Our groaning, our burden, our nakedness are our mortality. This knowledge is so beautiful. All that earthly, mortal, human stuff will be swallowed up. I can't wait. All that will be left will be life. Death will be gone. When we arrive in heaven, death will be swallowed up by life, and life will be all we see.

Death is going to be swallowed up by victory (1 Cor. 15:54). That knee that hurts will be swallowed up by victory. That anger will be swallowed up by victory. That impatience, that meanness, that fear, that grief, that bitterness, that broken relationship will all be swallowed up by life and victory. All that will remain is life. Let me say it again louder. This is not our final state. ALL THAT WILL REMAIN IS LIFE. Hallelujah!

Eternity is real, and reconciliation is eventual. Jesus wins. We will be reconciled. Would we prefer it happen here and now? Of course! However, more importantly, we know it will happen eventually. We will have a new building. We will have new clothes. We will have new life. We will have new relationships. Every injustice will be swallowed up by justice.

You may be saying, "Brian, I hear you, but I do not think the other person even knows Jesus, believes in Jesus, or has repented of their sin. I don't think we will be reconciled eventually. I don't think they are going to heaven. And what do I do for the next thirty or sixty years of our relationship?" I hear you. I've had the same thoughts.

That is all the more reason to bring them the gospel and to model the gospel. What did Jesus do for those who were sinners? What did he do for those far from God? What did he do for his enemies? Read the following passage, which explains what Christ has done for us. While reading, think about how God has done all of this for you, personally. Do not think you will do the same for the other person, because Jesus is the only one who can do these things. Yet, at the same time, understand that we are not to live in a way that contradicts what God has done.

> For while we were still helpless, at the right time Christ died for the ungodly. For one will hardly die for a righteous man; though perhaps for the good man someone would dare even to die. But God demonstrates His own love toward us, in that while we were yet sinners, Christ died for us. Much more then, having now been justified by His blood, we shall be saved from the wrath of God through Him. For if while we were enemies we were reconciled to God through the death of His Son, much more, having been reconciled, we shall be saved by His life. And not only this, but we also exult in God through our Lord Jesus Christ, through whom we have now received the reconciliation. (Rom. 5:6–11)

You are a Christian. You are a Christ-follower. The bottom line is that in your relationships in this world, you will need to, you will get to, and you are called to reflect the gospel. Jesus died for the ungodly, and we are called to die to self for those who do not know God. Dying to self includes laying down our rights and preferences, surrendering our will, and following God. We are not dying for their salvation but as an example to draw them to the cross. The gospel is both death and resurrection (1 Cor. 15:1–8). You have the opportunity to show others that you can die to yourself and walk in newness of life. You have the opportunity to model grace and truth. At your greatest point of injustice is your greatest opportunity for Christlikeness.

LIVING RECONCILED

Practical discoveries that will help you maintain reconciliation:

1. Conflict is inevitable, for we live in a fallen world.
2. Reconciliation is eventual. Seek to have an eternal perspective.

REVIEW AND RECAP

- In heaven, we will be completely new—bodies, emotions, desires, perceptions, attitudes. The wounds of the past will disappear. We will see through God's lens.
- We groan on earth simply because we have an absence of peace and safety. But we will have peace in heaven and freedom from anxiety.
- You are a Christian. You are a Christ-follower. In your relationships in this world, you are the reflection of the gospel.

He has made everything appropriate in its time. He has also set eternity in their heart, yet so that man will not find out the work which God has done from the beginning even to the end. (Eccl. 3:11)

Yet God has made everything beautiful for its own time. He has planted eternity in the human heart, but even so, people cannot see the whole scope of God's work from beginning to end. (v. 11 NLT)

TO MAKE YOU THINK

How does having a view of eternity change your view of your current conflict?

What will change in your broken relationships once you get to heaven?

Does anticipation of dwelling in heaven bring you joy? Why or why not?

What are you demanding now that may only get fixed once you are in heaven?

What would it look like to put on Jesus in your current conflict?

In your conflicted relationship, is death swallowing up life? Or is life swallowing up death?

3

≈

You Have Everything You Need

Have you heard the saying, "There are no guarantees in life except death and taxes"? That is so true! And there are definitely no guarantees of reconciliation here on earth. But what about in heaven? And what about God's guarantees? Let's look at the Word together. No matter what we go through here on earth, God guarantees he will be with us (Heb. 13:5). God promises he will go with us through the storm (Matt. 8:24). God pledges he will provide for us (6:26). God's Word declares he will not leave believers as orphans (John 14:18)—that includes being with us in our relationships.

A *guarantee* is a pledge. God gives us his Word as an unbreakable promise. God's Word is reliable and valid. And yes, I am talking about the Bible. The Bible is God's Word—his commitment, his pledge or guarantee to us. God's Word is truth. Sometimes our circumstances or experiences scream that God's Word is not true. However, I would much rather trust God's Word than my circumstances. Not only does God give us his Word (Ps. 119:105; Isa. 40:8; Matt. 24:35) but he has also given us his Spirit as his pledge.

Given a Pledge

> Now He who prepared us for this very purpose is God, who gave to us the Spirit as a pledge. (2 Cor. 5:5)

You have been prepared for a divine purpose. Yes, you! What is this "very purpose" Paul is talking about? Look back at verse 4: "For indeed while we are in this tent, we groan, being burdened, because we do not want to be unclothed but to be clothed, so that what is mortal will be swallowed up by life." The text says you have been prepared by God for the purpose of living out your human life even while longing to have your mortal self be swallowed up. That is why you groan. You can't wait for the changes coming from God. It can be frustrating at times to sit and wonder when and how things will change. I point you back to the Word of God: we live in the temporal; we live in the now. But hallelujah, one day what is mortal will be swallowed up by eternal life. How do we know that this is true? God has given us a pledge—a guarantee—of this truth in the form of the Holy Spirit.

Have you ever noticed that deep inside of you something brings hope? It isn't because you are a positive thinker. It is not because you are good. It is because, when you came to the point of surrendering your life to Jesus, the Holy Spirit came to reside in you.

What does it matter if the Holy Spirit is living inside of me? What does it matter if I have a pledge at all? Because it means you have everything you need to reconcile and to be reconciled.

When we are in relational conflict, we need something to grasp on to that enables us to keep seeking resolution. We need hope. The Holy Spirit is exactly that hope inside of you. This is the first of five pledges of the Holy Spirit: to give you hope.

Let's look at how John wrote about the pledge of the Holy Spirit. The Holy Spirit is your pledge of life (John 6:63). With the

Holy Spirit, even in the midst of relational death, you begin to rise above the storm. You begin to rise above the grave and know, feel, experience, and touch the very life of God; or rather, his life touches you. The same power that gave life to Jesus's body gives life to your mortal body (Rom. 8:11). The life of the resurrection is brand-new. We don't have decaying, dead stuff going on inside. In the core of our being, the Holy Spirit has been given, and where the Holy Spirit exists is life. That is awesome.

What's that? You don't feel life? The Holy Spirit is not a feeling. He is a pledge. You may say, "My thoughts are not full of life." The Holy Spirit is not positive thinking. He is a guarantee. Where Jesus resides, the Holy Spirit resides, and where the Holy Spirit resides is life. Proclaim the life of Jesus louder than the brokenness of your circumstances. Your circumstances may be your truth, but God's perspective on your circumstances is *the* truth.

I know this may be new to some of you. I understand that when we talk about our relationships, we have to include the reality of our actions, fallenness, and sinful behavior. However, you are not a slave to any of these things. You have a pledge to be empowered with the lifegiving flow of the Holy Spirit.

So, what do you want to use for getting through this difficult time? Do you want to focus on your fallenness, or do you want to focus on God's salvation, redemption, and newness that only come through the working of his Holy Spirit?

Here is what the Scriptures guarantee: in every believer dwells the Holy Spirit. Whatever the Spirit of God touches blossoms, grows, becomes fruitful, multiplies, and is brand-new. Yes, you are resurrected. Yes, you are new.

Even now, your heart may be screaming, *Wait a minute! I am not new. I am a sinner barely being justified by God.* Really? I don't think so. In fact, nowhere in Scripture does it say that. The Bible actually says believers—such as you and me—are saints (Phil. 4:21). Some will argue that Romans 7 says believers are still in sin. However, Romans 6 says we have been set free from the slavery of sin and are slaves of righteousness (vv. 17–18). Romans 8 says we are not obligated to sin but rather are putting to death the deeds of the flesh (vv. 12–13). Yes, we wrestle with sin, but we are wrestling not for salvation but sanctification.

What else comes through the Holy Spirit? The second pledge is *help* (John 14:16, 26; 15:26). As I come alongside others in their conflicts, I experience over and over their declarations that they can't forgive so-and-so for what they did. I tell them that I know they can't but the Holy Spirit can, and he is here to help us forgive. If forgiveness and reconciliation were based on our abilities as believers who are saved by grace through faith, we would all be in trouble. Forgiveness and reconciliation are based on Jesus Christ alone and his work on the cross, his work in the tomb, his work out of the tomb, and his work after the tomb (1 Cor. 15:1–8). Your ability doesn't matter. His ability does. He has given us each a pledge, a helper to aid us in our weaknesses. He himself is our forever helper (John 14:16).

Some may say, "I don't know how to pray. How do I get help?" It's okay if you don't know what to say. The Holy Spirit intercedes on our behalf—on your behalf, specifically (Rom. 8:26). And he not only intercedes on our behalf but helps us out and intercedes according to the will of God (v. 27). We all get so hung up on thinking we are a big deal. Guess what: we're not. The Holy Spirit inside each believer is a much bigger deal. You have the Holy Spirit, and the Holy Spirit is praying to the Father for you.

Does that mean we should not pray or have conversation with God? Of course not. Prayer is amazing because we get to simply talk to almighty God and connect directly with the Father. I am just encouraging you to remember God is bigger than your prayers, and the Spirit is interceding for you every moment you feel like you can't talk to God, don't know how to talk to God, forget to talk to God, or ignore God.

The third pledge of the Holy Spirit is his promise to abide in you, stay with you, and be available so that you can know him personally (John 14:17). Brace yourself; here we go on the Trinity. We don't serve three separate Gods. We serve one God (10:30). Where the Father is, Jesus is. Where Jesus is, the Holy Spirit is. Where the Holy Spirit is, the Father is. Why do I bring this up now? Most believers trust they have Jesus dwelling in them, but many don't recognize or believe this means the Holy Spirit abides with them and in them. This is like having a major power plant living inside of you and not realizing what you have. Can you imagine having the God of the universe living inside of you, giving you the power, ability, and resources to live in freedom? "Where the Spirit of the Lord is, there is freedom" (2 Cor. 3:17 NIV). Freedom abides with you and in you. Freedom from fear. Freedom from anxiety. Freedom from doubt. Freedom from broken relationships. From anger. From bitterness. You *are free*. You are free because the Holy Spirit dwells in you and with you. I don't guarantee it; I don't have to. God's guarantee is through his pledge of the Holy Spirit.

The fourth pledge is God's promise to teach you (John 14:26). The Holy Spirit is an amazing teacher. That means you can grow and learn in all things. He doesn't teach you only theology and then leave you in broken relationships. He, the Holy Spirit, teaches you humility, dying to self, and truth. This part of the pledge is amazing—the teacher is in you, teaching you. And this is not simply because we are failing. If I need to be taught, it means he understands that I have potential and room for *growth*. The Holy Spirit is the forever teacher. He is training you always. He is running drills and exercises and having you walk through scenarios to grow you. He is teaching you about God's peace (v. 27).

Finally, the fifth pledge of the Holy Spirit is to guide you into all truth (16:13). The Holy Spirit will never speak contrary to what the Father speaks. He doesn't speak of his own initiative. I love this. I know every morning when I sit down with the Bible, it is like the Spirit of God has a gigantic highlighter and is highlighting his Word for me—speaking directly to me. He is not shy. He guides me into the truth of God's Word. He looks deep into my heart and whispers, *Look there. You need that*. Recently, during my devotions, he showed me what gifts go with truth:

- grace and truth (John 1:14–17)
- Spirit and truth (John 4:23–24)
- testimony and truth (John 5:33)

- freedom and truth (John 8:32)
- way, truth, and life (John 14:6)

After compiling this list, I started thinking about why I see grace and truth as polarizing. Why do I so often think of grace *or* truth? There is no "either/or" in God's kingdom; it is a kingdom of grace *and* truth. But I often live in my relationships with grace or truth. Those Bible verses have been written for thousands of years, yet the Holy Spirit, through the Word of God, led me to see in them what I needed to see that day: Jesus is grace and truth. Jesus is the way, the truth, and the life.

This is an example of the pledge of the Holy Spirit working out in me. What is the character and work of the Holy Spirit? To guide us to truth. He speaks only the things he hears from the Father.

Simply put, as a believer in Jesus Christ, you are given a pledge. That pledge is in you and with you. That pledge is guiding you, helping you, teaching you, and empowering you. This is so important. If you want to live reconciled, it will not be based on your own willpower—it will be based on the Holy Spirit who dwells in you.

Take Courage

> Therefore, being always of good courage, and knowing that while we are at home in the body we are absent from the Lord—for we walk by faith, not by sight—we are of good courage, I say, and prefer rather to be absent from the body and to be at home with the Lord. (2 Cor. 5:6–8)

Since what is mortal is swallowed up by the resurrection life of Jesus—since we have the Holy Spirit as a pledge—therefore, we can be "always of good courage." I love the foundation Paul lays in this passage. It is critical knowledge. He doesn't say, "You: go conjure up courage." Paul does not tell us to self-motivate. He tells us to base our courage completely on Jesus Christ and the Holy Spirit.

There are days when I don't feel like being always of good courage. When we look at the Greek word we translate *always*, it means "at all times" or "perpetually." That is a huge challenge: at all times, perpetually, having courage. This is daunting if it is based on what we can personally do or on our works. That is why the context is key.

This "always" challenge is not based on you. It is not based on your abilities. It is based on Jesus and the Holy Spirit. Remember, it is okay to remind discouragement to get behind you. To stomp on its ugly head. Your life has been swallowed up with Christ's life. Your tent has been consumed with God's house. As a child of God, you are empowered by the Holy Spirit.

Courage can be defined as bold, confident hope in Jesus that brings about a cheerful heart at peace in the storms of life while we are in this world. Wow, that was a mouthful! But really think about it. We live in a fallen world, where many are discouraged. The Bible is full of verses that inspire us toward being encouraged and taking courage. I want to ask you to do something. Take the next three Bible verses and read them out loud two or three times. I have altered the verses (identified by the bold words) to make them a first-person experience.

The Lord is the one who goes ahead of **me**; He will be with **me**. He will not fail **me** or forsake **me**. **I will** not fear or be dismayed. (Deut. 31:8)

In **Jesus I will** have peace. In the world **I will** have tribulation, but **I will** take courage; **Jesus has** overcome the world. (John 16:33)

Now may the God of hope fill **me** with all joy and peace in believing, so that **I** will abound in hope by the power of the Holy Spirit. (Rom. 15:13)

Right now we are physically absent from the Lord. This is why it requires faith to walk with him. The day that we get to see and touch and smell and experience the fullness of his presence is going to be an awesome day. But though we are absent physically, we are not absent spiritually. He is with us—with me and also with you. He goes before us. At the same time, the Christian walk is a faith journey, not a sight journey. I know that in my relationships I want to physically see the promises of God, and no doubt you also desire that. Faith journeying is a hard concept to fully comprehend. Yet we are on such a journey. We trust even when we don't see. I want to encourage you to have faith even when you don't have sight.

We are of good courage and prefer to be at home with Jesus. Some question how we can be of good courage when we can't see. That is exactly what faith is! Faith replaces sight. So, if faith is the replacement for sight, is faith blind? Yes and no. We might be unable to physically see the Lord, but our spiritual senses—touching, tasting, hearing, smelling, and seeing—are fully functional. We can taste and see that the Lord is good (Ps. 34:8). We can touch God because the Holy Spirit touches our spirit (Rom. 8:16–17). Our spiritual eyes have seen God (2 Cor. 4:6). We hear the voice of Jesus (John 10:27). I am, however, not sure about spiritually smelling Jesus. (Joke, people; I'm joking.) And yet, while I am not aware of any verses where we smell Jesus, I do know the Old Testament says that sacrifices are a pleasant smell to him (Gen. 8:21; Exod. 29:18; Lev. 1:9). Olfactory theology aside, my main point here is that our senses are involved in encountering God through his Word and through the Holy Spirit.

You might be in a conflict this very moment and need reconciliation. I guarantee if you encounter God through his Word, it will change how you respond to the other people in your conflict. In fact, an authentic encounter with God has changed people instantaneously for generations. Abraham encountered God, and he was changed forever. Moses encountered God, and his limited abilities were used by God miraculously. Joseph experienced injustice after injustice, and his perspective completely changed. Job was challenged, and God delivered him. Peter hung out and ministered with Jesus, and he was changed forever. Paul met up with Jesus on the road, and he did a one-eighty. If God's Word is allowed to shape and reshape your present perspective, you will embrace reconciliation no matter how the other person responds.

You can't encounter God through his Word and not be changed. Take courage, and in your courage, please the Lord.

Pleasing to Him

> Therefore we also have as our ambition, whether at home or absent, to be pleasing to Him. For we must all appear before the judgment seat of Christ, so that each one may be recompensed for his deeds in the body, according to what he has done, whether good or bad. (2 Cor. 5:9–10)

In your journey toward reconciliation or to maintain reconciliation, what is your ambition? To be right? Or to be reconciled? This is a big question. I know when I am in conflict with my spouse or kids, often I have a stronger desire to be right than to be reconciled. Think about it. If Jesus desired to be right more than he desired to be reconciled, and he was 100 percent right, he would have never gone to the cross (1 Pet. 2:22). The fact is that Jesus desired to be reconciled way more than he desired to declare his sinlessness, righteousness, or right-ness (Rom. 5:8). Reconciliation was his whole ambition. His motivation was to die for sinners. We call ourselves Christ-followers; however, often when we're in conflict we don't want to follow in Christ's footsteps. We—okay, fine, I'll keep it personal—I only want to apologize for those behaviors I intentionally, willfully, and premeditatedly do against someone else. The fact is, if Jesus had that same attitude toward me, I would be stuck in my sin. Let's make our ambition match Jesus's ambition. He died—for reconciliation.

As followers of Jesus, whether we are on earth or in heaven, to be pleasing to Jesus truly needs to be our ambition. This focus includes our conflicts. It is very easy to look at these verses from 2 Corinthians in a vacuum, absent practical daily living. It is easy to think, *Well, in my religious practices, of course I want to please him, but in my relationships, my friendships, my marriage, my parenting, or whatever else I encounter, I am not sure it is that important.* But Paul's next statement says something compelling to push us to be pleasing to Christ: "We must all appear before the judgment seat of Christ" (2 Cor. 5:10). It is hard for us to imagine this day of judgment before Christ. What will it be like for the unbeliever? What will it be like for the believer? Scripture clearly connects having an ambition that pleases Jesus to the judgment of Jesus. Let's look at the verse a little closer from some other versions of the Bible.

> For we must all appear before the judgment seat of Christ, so that each one may receive what is due for what he has done in the body, whether good or evil. (v. 10 ESV)

> Sooner or later we'll all have to face God, regardless of our conditions. We will appear before Christ and take what's coming to us as a result of our actions, either good or bad. (v. 10 Message)

God cares about how we handle our earthly relationships. He cares about our earthly actions. He places our relationships with each other in the top two greatest commandments. I can't imagine that on judgment day we won't give an account as to how we have loved him and how we have loved others. I know we don't like to hear this, but our conflicts matter to God. Our responses to others matter to God, and our actions matter too. Personally, I know I will need God's grace in weighing out my responses to injustices and to conflict. I tend to overreact and respond poorly to others. I have grown, but I have a ways to go. I also know that I am saved by grace, kept by grace, and restored by grace.

The steps we take to reconcile with others are important. I often can get focused on the temporal, the here and now, the earthly or fallen stuff. I need to learn to shut my mouth and listen. I need to grow in having a humble heart that truly trusts in God. I often pray that my actions will glorify him. My ambition is to see my relationships and situations through a lens of hope, not despair. Let me model a simple prayer to reinforce this and ask God for help.

Lord, you are amazing. I am in a situation where conflict seems to be at every turn. I am looking at my life, and it seems hopeless. Lord, I have been selfish and have tried to serve and protect myself. I have tried to justify myself. The truth is that you are my protector. You are my justifier. Help me to have an approachable attitude and actions. Help me to be teachable. Help me to allow others to speak into my life. In Jesus's name, amen.

Sincere Heart

Therefore, knowing the fear of the Lord, we persuade men, but we are made manifest to God; and I hope that we are made manifest also in your consciences. We are not again commending ourselves to you but are giving you an occasion to be proud of us, so that you will have an answer for those who take pride in appearance and not in heart. (2 Cor. 5:11–12)

Did you notice that this is the third "therefore" in this passage? Let's lay these out, because it will really enable us to grasp the message of the Scripture. The Holy Spirit is given to believers as a pledge (v. 5), and

1. *Therefore*, be of good courage.
2. *Therefore*, have an ambition to please God.
3. *Therefore*, know the fear of the Lord.

There is so much depth in these verses. Let's start with "the fear of the Lord." What does it mean to fear the Lord? Why do we need to fear him? Does fearing God involve insecurity or threat? If he is a loving God, why should we fear him?

We fear the Lord because he impartially judges everyone according to our works on earth (1 Pet. 1:17). The impartiality of God is something we wrestle with. We want God to impartially judge our adversary, our enemy, or the person we are in conflict with. However, we want him to judge *us* with grace and mercy. The fact is, on the day of judgment, we will all experience God's impartiality. He will treat everyone the same. God's judgments are true and righteous (Ps. 19:9). The believer will be seen through the blood of Christ and yet justice will be served, both the injustices we have caused and the injustices we have experienced. As believers, we should not be flippant about standing before God. God takes forgiveness very seriously (Matt. 18:21–34; Mark 11:25). We must realize that if we practice breaking relationships, neither care nor repent, or wrestle with honoring God, God doesn't wink at willful disobedience (Matt. 7:21–23; Heb. 6:4–6; 10:26–31; James 4:17; 1 John 5:3). I am not trying to depress you or guilt you into obeying God. Rather I am trying to encourage you to have a holy fear and reverence for his impartiality.

Our willingness to be a reconciler is important. Maintaining reconciliation and living reconciled are equally essential. A critical part of reconciliation is a sincere heart. Some want to reconcile for appearance's sake. They want to look good, but internally they hate their enemy. I am sure that is not you, but I need to address this just to make sure we are all clear about this concept. Sometimes, we carry around bitterness, anger, and malice (Eph. 4:31). We must be willing to let go of this stuff, this sin. You might be tempted to claim you can't change how you feel about someone else. Or you might protest that your thoughts keep getting the best of you. I understand. Remember, just because you have a feeling or a thought doesn't make it true. One hundred times a day, you might need to remind your inner fallenness that, because of the gospel, you choose to forgive the way Jesus has forgiven you (v. 32). You might need to take hold of your thoughts, your feelings, and your desires and remind them that you have forgiven because of Jesus's death on the cross (2 Cor. 10:5).

Your desires can align with, or become obedient to, Scripture. Look at the psalmist, who takes control of his desires and begins to look to the Lord for his help (Ps. 121). You are a slave of the one you obey (Rom. 6:16–17), so obey the Word. You are not a victim. Take control of your heart and surrender it to Jesus. Take control of your inner self, command yourself to place your hope in God (Ps. 42:5), and begin to praise God again. Reconciliation is not for the purpose of looking good but to really do the will of God (Eph. 6:6).

I like to ask myself, *How long do I really want a conflict to steal my joy? Do I truly want reconciliation?* If I do, then I have to decipher how that reconciliation is possible. Reconciliation is possible only because of the gospel, and Jesus tells us to pick up our cross daily and follow him. So if I want reconciliation, I must ask myself, from a sincere heart, *To what do I need to die?* Then, through Scripture reading and prayer, I must take control of my heart and command it to align with God's Word and the Holy Spirit. What motivates me is God's love, and what keeps me motivated is God's impartiality and knowing I will stand before him one day and give an account of my life and my choices. My relationship with him is based on both reverence and love.

As we wrap up this chapter, remember this simple truth: the Holy Spirit dwells within you and is empowering you to glorify God. You can be the reconciler God has called you to be because of Jesus.

LIVING RECONCILED

Practical discoveries that will help you maintain reconciliation:

1. Conflict is inevitable, for we live in a fallen world.
2. Reconciliation is eventual. Seek to have an eternal perspective.
3. You have been given a pledge: you have the Holy Spirit to help you reconcile.

REVIEW AND RECAP

- God pledges to provide what you need—the Holy Spirit—who will:
  1. Give you hope.
  2. Help you.

3. Abide in/with you.

4. Teach you and guide you to truth.

- A critical part of reconciliation is a sincere heart.

Grace and peace be multiplied to you in the knowledge of God and of Jesus our Lord; seeing that His divine power has granted to us everything pertaining to life and godliness, through the true knowledge of Him who called us by His own glory and excellence. For by these He has granted to us His precious and magnificent promises, so that by them you may become partakers of the divine nature, having escaped the corruption that is in the world by lust. Now for this very reason also, applying all diligence, in your faith supply moral excellence, and in your moral excellence, knowledge, and in your knowledge, self-control, and in your self-control, perseverance, and in your perseverance, godliness, and in your godliness, brotherly kindness, and in your brotherly kindness, love. For if these qualities are yours and are increasing, they render you neither useless nor unfruitful in the true knowledge of our Lord Jesus Christ. For he who lacks these qualities is blind or short-sighted, having forgotten his purification from his former sins. (2 Pet. 1:2–9)

TO MAKE YOU THINK

How does knowing the Holy Spirit is dwelling in you bring you hope?

How does knowing the Holy Spirit is empowering you give you confidence?

Since God's divine power has given you everything you need to live a godly life, how might that reshape your response to your present conflict? (Look at 2 Pet. 1:3 above.)

How might you apply diligence to glorify God in this
conflict?

What role does self-control need to have as you move through
your present conflict?

What are a few action items you can take to maintain
perseverance?

4

Go Crazy for God's Glory

Let's learn how to be faithful during our tension so that God is honored and glorified. I understand that conflict and the desire for reconciliation can often be overwhelming. They can also be so devastating we begin to believe we are not going to make it through the situation.

But I know a truth for each of us—for you. Jesus is in your boat (Mark 4:38–40), or maybe more accurately, you are in Jesus's boat. You will make it to the other side. How can I be so sure? It is simple. I don't need to know your abilities or even your situation. I know the Jesus inside of you, who said you are going to the other side of the lake (Matt. 8:23–27). Jesus will be with you in your storm. Jesus will calm your storm. It may not happen here on earth, but I guarantee it will happen in heaven.

It is important to focus on each day as it comes. It is critical to not allow yourself to worry about tomorrow (6:25–34). Rather, in your relationships and in your conflict, begin to honor God today. Speculation about how the other person may respond to your behavior change will try to creep up on you, but it will not do you any good. Calm down the desire to self-justify and make excuses for your behavior, your responses, and your motives. God is your justifier (Rom. 8:33). You have an opportunity to glorify God (1 Cor. 10:31). Focus on that and not on the storm. Day by day. Hour by hour. Minute by minute. Even second by second, if that's what you need to stay on mission.

But how? What does it mean, practically, to glorify God? It means to *show it*. It means to be all in. It means, well, going crazy for God's glory. Not crazy like out-of-our-mind crazy, but crazy as in extremely enthusiastic. God is extremely enthusiastic about reconciling the world to himself through Jesus Christ (Col. 1:19–20). So why wouldn't we be enthusiastically crazy for reconciliation too?

> For if we are beside ourselves, it is for God; if we are of sound mind, it is for you. (2 Cor. 5:13)

"For if we are beside ourselves." What does that mean? Well, when in doubt, I look at a few different translations of the Bible. In *The Message* paraphrase, verse 13 reads, "If I acted crazy, I did it for God; if I acted overly serious, I did it for you." The world might see our extremely enthusiastic behavior for the gospel as being the out-of-our-mind type of crazy. But even if we are out of our minds, it is for God.

This is such a unique set of verses. Paul is clear here that if we are going mad, it is for God's glory. The gospel is worth becoming zealous for; Jesus is worthy of extremely enthusiastic behavior. We are not the frozen chosen. We are not the cold cobblers (though I don't even know what that means). We are children of God. We have a great mission. We are here to see people transformed by the gospel. Here is the key: the world will have a hard time believing the gospel if our relationships are unreconciled and in the pit. So before looking into reconciliation, we must understand both what the gospel is and also what it means to go crazy for it—and go crazy for God.

The Gospel

The gospel, the good news of Jesus Christ, is woven throughout Scripture from Genesis to Revelation; however, the most precise and concise description is presented by Paul in 1 Corinthians 15:3–8:

> For I delivered to you as of first importance what I also received, that *Christ died* for our sins according to the Scriptures, and that *He was buried*, and that *He was raised* on the third day according to the Scriptures, and that *He appeared* to Cephas, then to the twelve. After that He appeared to more than five hundred brethren at one time, most of whom remain until now, but some have fallen asleep; then He appeared to James, then to all the apostles; and last of all, as to one untimely born, He appeared to me also.

The phrase "of first importance" is extremely significant. When the Bible says that of all the things being said, this one thing is of "first importance," we need to wake up, pay attention, and look closely. Paul delivered this important message to the Corinthians and now to us. He said Jesus died, was buried, rose, and appeared. These four words, if lived out daily, will change, challenge, and ultimately allow you to reconcile your relationships. Let me say them again, a little louder: DEATH—BURIAL—RESURRECTION—APPEARANCE.

There is only one gospel, and it has always been consistent through all of history. The gospel that reconciles you to God is the same gospel that reconciles your relationships here on earth.

Let's reexamine a Scripture we discussed earlier:

> And He was saying to them all, "If anyone wishes to come after Me, he must deny himself, and take up his cross daily and follow Me." (Luke 9:23)

This passage refers to the same daily gospel that saves you. The same daily death, burial, resurrection, and appearance that sanctify you. I am in no way suggesting you must die to save others;

I am saying you must pick up your cross daily and follow Jesus because he *did* die for them. I am not saying salvation is a daily event, as if you fall in and out of salvation. I am saying salvation includes a daily sanctification, a daily denying of yourself, a daily taking up of your cross and following Jesus's example of death, burial, resurrection, and appearance.

The gospel pairs two actions with two evidences, or proofs, of these actions. The evidence of death is burial. The evidence of resurrection is appearance. For example, if I claim to have resurrected from the dead and yet never show myself to anyone, why would I be believed? Or if I claim someone has died and yet can give no evidence of having buried them, questions will come up about whether or not that person ever truly died.

To fully live the gospel, we must understand what its message is—at least as far as humanly possible. So let's look more closely at each step of the gospel as outlined in 1 Corinthians 15:3–8.

Gospel Action #1: Death

> For I delivered to you as of first importance what I also received, that *Christ died* for our sins according to the Scriptures. (1 Cor. 15:3)

The death of Jesus is one of the most important actions predicted in the Old Testament (Ps. 22; Isa. 53:3–7; Zech. 11:12). Jesus was 100 percent sinless, 100 percent righteous, and 100 percent holy, and yet he died a sinner's death. It seems to me if there were any other way to pay for the penalty of sin, he would have done it. However, the act of sacrificial death is the only act that pays for sin (Rom. 5:8; Gal. 3:13; 1 Pet. 2:24; 1 John 2:2).

Just as Christ died for us, we need to learn to die to ourselves. Die to our sinful nature. Die to broken relationships. Die to being right. Die to being self-justified. I see, over and over, Christians who desire to be vindicated on this side of heaven. They take vengeance into their own hands. But God calls them to die to their own vengeful desires and let him handle vengeance (Deut.

32:35; Rom. 12:19). Romans 6 alone includes an extensive list of death statements that clearly identify we are to die with Jesus and hide our lives with him. While I list below only the specific related points, I encourage you to read the entire text. Believers in Jesus

- have died to sin (v. 2).
- have been baptized into his death (v. 3).
- are united with Jesus in the likeness of his death (v. 4).
- have allowed their old self to be crucified with Jesus (v. 6).
- are dead to sin (v. 11).
- are not mastered by sin (v. 14).

Gospel Evidence #1: Burial

And that *He was buried*, and that He was raised on the third day according to the Scriptures. (1 Cor. 15:4)

Burial is the evidence of being dead. When someone dies, you bury them. Burial shows finality. In your relationships, when you repent and commit to change, you are burying sin. When you show that you no longer walk in your previous sinful ways, you are giving evidence of God's work in your life.

Burying living things is not good. In the same way, simply burying poor behavior you are not willing to repent of or turn from, or pretending you are changed, is not healthy. Burial is not about stuffing behaviors down and acting like they did not happen. Burial is authentic repentance that acknowledges sinful behavior or hurt caused and asks for forgiveness with a commitment to change. So much of our gospel presentation these days is missing the evidence portion of the message.

Gravedigging is not advised. When God forgives your sin, he removes it as far as the east is from the west (Ps. 103:12). In other words, he doesn't go gravedigging. Old bitterness stinks to high heaven. Old resentment is a rotting corpse. Dead anger is a decaying body. Stop going back to those things. Repent and leave them in the grave. Believers in Jesus

- have buried their sin with Jesus (Rom. 6:4).
- know their sinful body has been done away with (v. 6).

You have been buried with Jesus. This is some of the most beautiful imagery we have in the Scriptures. You will not die alone. You will not be buried alone. The burial, the tomb, that Jesus experienced is the same we experience at salvation. I know in our physical, earthly minds this is hard to comprehend. However, it still is true. You have been buried with Jesus.

Gospel Action #2: Resurrection

And that He was buried, and that *He was raised* on the third day according to the Scriptures. (1 Cor. 15:4)

The newness that comes from the gospel is missing from most relationships, both in the church and in our daily lives. Yet we are no longer slaves to sin. We are no longer jerks. We are no longer angry or depressed men and women. We are brand-new—we are resurrected with Christ.

This resurrection is both in our relationships with God and with others. However, we like to make excuses for our flesh so that we do not have to be responsible for our bad behavior. And yet, in our resurrection with Christ, we are brand-new. Let me say it again. YOU ARE BRAND-NEW. I know I am yelling; I just can't contain it. Go back to Romans 6. Believers in Jesus

- are resurrected (v. 4).
- are united with Jesus in a resurrection like his (v. 5).
- have been raised from the dead (v. 9).
- are alive to God in Christ (v. 11).

The old no longer holds true. The new you can interact in righteousness both toward God and toward others. I get so tired of people saying they can't change but they expect others to change. We have a tendency to excuse our own sinful wrestling while judging others'. You are enslaved to God. Your body is new and belongs to him. So walk in that newness.

Jesus's resurrection changed everything. He conquered death. He overcame sin. He paid the price for humanity. Sinless became sin and then conquered sin by resurrecting. The resurrection forced death to no longer be our master. That is amazing. We don't have to sit in fear and frustration. We can dust ourselves off, walk in newness, and out-love others.

Gospel Evidence #2: Appearance

> *He appeared* to Cephas, then to the twelve. After that He appeared to more than five hundred brethren at one time, most of whom remain until now, but some have fallen asleep; then He appeared to James, then to all the apostles; and last of all, as to one untimely born, He appeared to me also. (1 Cor. 15:5–8)

Just like burial is the evidence of death, appearance is the evidence of resurrection. After being resurrected, Jesus showed himself to over five hundred people. Think about that: we have five hundred individual testimonies of Jesus's resurrection. Five hundred separate people who clearly identified seeing the resurrected Jesus, the sinless man with a physically risen body who presented himself as righteous before God and people. How does that apply to us? Believers in Jesus

- do not continue in sin (Rom. 6:1–2).
- live a new life (v. 4).
- offer themselves to God as those brought to life from death (v. 13).
- are slaves to righteousness (v. 18).
- are God's slaves (v. 22).

Too many Christ-followers say they are following Christ but lack the evidence of newness of life. In fact, it is not just those other people; that evidence is also lacking in me. The greatest evidence of a changed life, a resurrected life, is the fruit of the Holy Spirit. Love enters into our relationships. Joy springs up. Peace washes over us. Patience takes its rightful place. Kindness is evident. Gentleness is present. Faithfulness surrounds. Self-control takes center stage. Goodness is lived out. We, or at least I, need to allow the Holy Spirit to move and shape this newness of life.

Embracing the Gospel for God's Glory

The gospel is foolishness to the world (1 Cor. 1:18). When you truly embrace the gospel in your relationships, some will think you have gone crazy. The gospel, in and of itself, will not make sense to others. The gospel is for salvation and the gospel is for sanctification—daily refinement.

> Then he said to the crowd, "If any of you wants to be my follower, you must give up your own way, take up your cross daily, and follow me." (Luke 9:23 NLT)

Taking up your cross and following Jesus is a daily opportunity. Notice what Jesus makes this action conditional upon. He says that if anyone desires to come after him—to follow in his footsteps (literally to be a Christ-follower or Christian)—they will end up at death on the cross, burial in a tomb, resurrection from the tomb, and then showing themselves to Christ's disciples and many others as well (1 Cor. 15:1–9). Those results are our four basic concepts: death—burial—resurrection—appearance. Again, these four words are critical; if Jesus hasn't placed this same gospel inside of you, none of the other things I am going to share are going to matter. Willpower will not transform you; only gospel-resurrection power can transform. Let's walk through 1 Corinthians 15 slowly to ensure we clearly understand this concept of *gospel*, which is so key to reconciliation.

Preach the Gospel

Now I make known to you, brethren, the gospel which I preached to you. (1 Cor. 15:1)

The gospel is preached through our words (Rom. 10:14). The gospel is preached through our actions (1 John 3:18). The gospel is preached through our interactions (John 13:35). The gospel is preached through our conflicts, tensions, and reconciliations. Some might think that either words, actions, or interactions are the most important, but the reality is we need all these pieces in alignment. We don't wait until we have the action and evidence of the gospel perfect in our lives to begin sharing the message. The greatness about the gospel is that it uses our weaknesses to accomplish its purpose (2 Cor. 12:9).

Receive the Gospel

Which also you received. (1 Cor. 15:1)

The gospel is received by faith and kept by faith (Gal. 2:16). It is God's gift (Rom. 3:24). If we confess Jesus as Lord and believe that God raised him from the dead, we receive the gospel and are saved (10:9). We are not receiving human words but God's Word (1 Thess. 2:13). The gospel is implanted in those who receive it (James 1:21).

Stand in the Gospel

In which also you stand. (1 Cor. 15:1)

Standing in the gospel is a unique and interesting way of thinking about our interactions with it. The Greek word for stand, *hístēmi*, can also mean placed, caused to stand, or set.[1] Jesus told a parable about a man who built his house on the rock and a man who built his house on the sand (Matt. 7:24–27). One man took his stand on the gospel, and one took his stand on the world. The one who acts on the words of Jesus has a foundation that is firm; the one who acts on the words of the world will fall.

Be Saved by the Gospel
By which also you are saved. (1 Cor. 15:2)

The only thing that will save us is the gospel. From what are we being saved? Scripturally, the wages of sin is death (Rom. 6:23). Hell is a real place to which we go to serve out that death sentence from sin; therefore, the gospel saves us from eternal punishment (Matt. 25:46). We are saved from "the lake that burns with fire and brimstone, which is the second death" (Rev. 21:8). We are literally saved from hell.

Hold Fast to the Gospel
If you hold fast the word which I preached to you. (1 Cor. 15:2)

Look at this verse closely. It specifically says that believers must hold fast to the gospel. Ultimately the gospel is holding on to us, but at the same time, we are to cling to the gospel. Here is what I find more often than not when it comes to conflict: the believer's theoretical, theological knowledge is accurate and biblically correct; however, their application of that knowledge is far from the message of the gospel. It is critical to our communities that the gospel move out from the four walls of our churches and into our relationships on the streets. We do this by holding fast to the gospel in practical ways.

Remember, you can hold fast to your rights. You can hold fast to being self-justified. You can hold fast to your image and your name. You can hold fast to your reputation. You can hold fast to a lot of things. That does not mean you are holding fast to the humble gospel, the gospel of the cross, the gospel of the Messiah. Look at your hand. What are you holding on to? Are you holding on to anger, bitterness, wrath, vengeance, slander, or speculation? Are you holding on to fear, annoyance, hurt, the past, or self-justification? What is it? And if you are holding on to these things, how do you have room to cling to the gospel?

Reject Vain Belief in the Gospel
Unless you believed in vain. (1 Cor. 15:2)

The reality is that many followers of Jesus, including me, will say we are Christ-followers, but we want to follow Jesus every-where but to the cross. When we are willing to follow Jesus in miracles, in healing, in providing, in comforting, and in disciplin-ing, yet not follow him to the cross, our belief is in vain. Everything in the life of Jesus brought him to the point of the cross.

It is vain to claim Jesus is Lord of your worship and yet deny him as Lord of your relationships. The gospel that causes you to love God is the same gospel that causes you to love others. The gospel that reconciles you to God is the same gospel that reconciles you to others.

I think we will be surprised when we get to heaven to discover how much of our walk with God was rooted in vanity. We have great claims but little action. Not that our actions save us. Nor do our interactions. However, the gospel is meant to be the center of both our actions and interactions.

Going Crazy for God

Now that we've established what the gospel message is all about and how it should shape and define all believers, let's return to 2 Corinthians 5:13: "For if we are beside ourselves, it is for God; if we are of sound mind, it is for you." This verse is looking at the same coin from two different sides:

1. If you think we are crazy or beside ourselves—well, that is for God.
2. You might think we are of sound mind or are acting overly serious—and that is for you.

People sometimes think that if believers are completely sold out to honoring God with their lives and in their relationships, those believers must be out of their minds. However, Paul appears to be saying that even though the world sees sold-out believers as loony for Jesus, God simply recognizes this as being extremely enthusiastic for him. Let's look at a few Old Testament and New Testament examples of believers who were crazy for God.

Noah Was Crazy for God's Glory

Noah lived in a time when the earth was becoming more and more corrupt. Sin was increasingly abounding in society. God saw Noah was a crazy man who was extremely enthusiastic about serving him. Scripture says Noah was a righteous man, blameless in his time, who walked with God (Gen. 6:9).

God put Noah on a mission to demonstrate God's grace and ultimately the gospel. He had Noah build an ark—not just a little rowboat but a huge ship (vv. 14–15). Now that is nuts. However, God said he was going to flood the earth, and only Noah and those along with him in the ark would be saved. Noah obeyed God and started building (v. 22).

That kind of obedience requires an absurd, crazy, or extremely enthusiastic desire to glorify God. After the ark was finished, God then sent animals two by two into it before he flooded the earth. And just like God promised, Noah and all his family were saved.

So, how does Noah's crazy, enthusiastic obedience apply to believers today? How can you relate? God isn't asking you to build an ark. God isn't asking you to do the impossible. He is asking you to be obedient to his Word: to forgive the way Jesus forgave, exercise humility, and trust him. Yes, like in Noah's day, this world is flooded with fallenness; God has promised to be with you during the storm.

Abraham Was Crazy for God's Glory

Abram (Abraham) was married to Sarai (Sarah), who was barren (Gen. 11:29–32). Yet God made a crazy promise to Abraham that he would father a great nation (12:1–3). Now, think about that for a minute. Abraham and Sarah couldn't have children, yet God promised he was going to make Abraham into an entire nation—and not a tiny little one but a *great* nation! That was impossible. That was not happening. That was crazy talk.

Abraham did a lot of things to try to have children. At Sarah's urging, he even had sex with another woman, Hagar (16:1–4). This was Abraham and Sarah trying to make God's promise happen in their own strength. God didn't need their help. He had to step in and remind Abraham of his promise (18:9–15). And eventually, God did fulfill his promise (21:1–3).

After all this, God made a crazy request of Abraham that did not make sense. However, God doesn't use human wisdom to accomplish his eternal purposes. God told Abraham to sacrifice his son on the altar (22:1–2). That's right! God asked him to sacrifice—to kill—the very fulfilled promise he had just given to Abraham. That is mind-boggling.

Yet Abraham began to do as God commanded. Why would he do that? Well, in the New Testament, we are shown that Abraham believed God would raise his son from the dead (Heb. 11:17–19). How is it possible that Abraham believed in the resurrection of the gospel, when he lived so many years before Jesus came to earth? Because the gospel message was preached to Abraham (Gal. 3:6–8), and Abraham trusted God even when it seemed crazy to do so.

Now, before you sacrifice your kids on the altar, understand that God then provided a ram in the bushes to be the substitute sacrifice (Gen. 22:11–14). Abraham did not actually kill his son. In this same way, God has provided you and me with a substitute sacrifice—and that sacrifice's name is Jesus.

Joseph Was Crazy for God's Glory

Joseph had some relational tension. His family hated him, his employer falsely accused him, and his friends forgot him (Gen. 37, 39). Yet God put him in a place of leadership (Gen. 41:38–45). When his family came to get help from him because of a famine, Joseph could have held a grudge and been bitter, resentful, and unforgiving. However, he demonstrated a crazy love for God by drawing his brothers closer and looking at his situation from an eternal perspective (45:4–8). Then he reached out to his family and took care of them for many years. But even then his brothers felt insecure in the relationship and told Joseph a concocted story to hopefully find favor with him. Despite this continued conflict-inducing behavior, Joseph still showed crazy reconciliation in Genesis 50.

> But Joseph said to them, "Do not be afraid, for am I in God's place? As for you, you meant evil against me, but God meant it for good in order to bring about this present result, to preserve many people alive. So therefore, do not be afraid; I will provide for you and your little ones." So he comforted them and spoke kindly to them. (vv. 19–21)

Joseph was amazingly crazy for God's glory. He comforted those who had hurt him and proved himself truly reconciled year after year. Wow! I need to learn from Joseph.

Zacharias and Elizabeth Were Crazy for God's Glory

The story of Zacharias and Elizabeth may be a less obvious example of going crazy for God's glory. They were the parents of John the Baptist. For many years, they could not conceive a child, and yet

> they were both righteous in the sight of God, walking blamelessly in all the commandments and requirements of the Lord. (Luke 1:6)

I don't know about you, but if I were mentioned in the Scriptures, I would love to be described as "righteous in the sight of God" and have it said of me that I "[walked] blamelessly in all of the commandments and requirements of the Lord." These people must have been crazy, sold out for God.

The Woman of Samaria Was (Eventually) Crazy for God's Glory

In this story, Jesus sat next to Jacob's well. He was weary from his journey (John 4:6). A woman of Samaria came to the well to get some water, and a conversation developed between her and Jesus about water, living water, her husband, and worship (vv. 7–24).

Jesus revealed to the woman that he was the Messiah (vv. 25–26). The woman, in response, went and told the people of Samaria whom it was she met (vv. 28–30). Many people believed in Jesus because of the testimony of the woman, which led them to their own firsthand experience with Jesus (vv. 39–42).

This woman did an amazing thing by simply pointing people to the Messiah. She didn't look at her lifestyle and use that as an excuse to not say anything about Jesus. She simply did what was right. She got crazy for God, and it changed the hearts and minds of others—not because of the absence of her past but despite her past.

The Woman with Perfume Was Crazy for God's Glory

A Pharisee invited Jesus over to his house to have dinner. Although we don't know the Pharisee's exact motive, we do know that he judged Jesus and the encounter Jesus had with a woman during this visit (Luke 7:39). This woman, a city-dwelling sinner, heard about Jesus being at the Pharisee's house. She took a bold step, a crazy step, especially given the culture of her day, showing up at the religious leader's house with an expensive vial of perfume. She then poured the perfume all over Jesus's feet—anointing him (vv. 37–38).

Jesus then told the Pharisee a story about two debtors who both owed money that was forgiven. He asked the Pharisee a question as to which would have more love for the one who forgave them their debts. The Pharisee answered correctly: the one with the bigger debt. Jesus then forgave the sins of the woman (v. 48).

Isn't that amazing? This woman took one crazy step toward Jesus, and Jesus poured out crazy forgiveness on her. I love this story.

The Boy with the Loaves and Fishes Was Crazy for God's Glory

One young boy gave his lunch to Jesus, who then used it to feed over five thousand people (John 6:1–14). We really don't know the entirety of this story, as not many details are given. We do know that somehow Andrew discovered the fish and bread this boy had brought for his lunch. We can probably assume Andrew didn't tackle the kid and take it from him; therefore, we must then assume the boy offered his lunch to Jesus. It seems reasonable to me that the kid had a childlike faith. He may have simply believed he should share what he had. Or maybe Jesus asked the boy if he could use it. Whatever the case, when comparing the quantity of food versus the huge number of people, it is crazy to think this boy's lunch would even make a dent in filling people's stomachs. However, Jesus used this offering and multiplied it—so much so that there were even leftovers. Such crazy math can only come from God. Wouldn't it be fascinating to know what happened to that boy who shared his lunch, and the impact his crazy generosity had on his own life?

~~~

Going crazy for the gospel—going crazy for the glory of the Lord—leads to changed people and changed relationships. If we want to be restored to others, we must start with understanding the gospel message for both ourselves and everyone else. And then we must consider letting go of our personal pride and hesitation and simply going crazy for the promises the Lord has given us in his Word. In the next several chapters, I am going to suggest attitudes you can use for maintaining reconciliation and daily living it out. These courageous attitudes are grounded in the message of the gospel, and each will challenge you both in your relationship with God and your relationships with others.

LIVING RECONCILED

Practical discoveries that will help you maintain reconciliation:

1. Conflict is inevitable, for we live in a fallen world.
2. Reconciliation is eventual. Seek to have an eternal perspective.

3. You have been given a pledge: you have the Holy Spirit to help you reconcile.

4. The gospel is real. Through the gospel message, you are emboldened to go crazy to glorify God.

REVIEW AND RECAP

- The world will have a hard time believing the gospel if our relationships are unreconciled and in the pit. It is vain to claim Jesus as Lord of your worship and yet deny him as Lord of your relationships.

- You can hold fast to being self-justified. You can hold fast to image and your name. You can hold fast to reputation. And if you are holding on to these things, how do you have room to cling to the gospel?

- God isn't asking you to do the impossible. He is asking you to be obedient to his Word: to forgive the way Jesus forgave, exercise humility, and trust him.

What shall we say then? Are we to continue in sin so that grace may increase? May it never be! How shall we who died to sin still live in it? Or do you not know that all of us who have been baptized into Christ Jesus have been baptized into His death? Therefore we have been buried with Him through baptism into death, so that as Christ was raised from the dead through the glory of the Father, so we too might walk in newness of life. For if we have become united with Him in the likeness of His death, certainly we shall also be in the likeness of His resurrection, knowing this, that our old self was crucified with Him, in order that our body of sin might be done away with, so that we would no longer be slaves to sin; for he who has died is freed from sin. Now if we have died with Christ, we believe that we shall also live with Him, knowing that Christ, having been raised from the dead, is never to die again; death no longer is master over Him. (Rom. 6:1–9)

TO MAKE YOU THINK

Death. I know such thoughts are crazy to consider, but what do *you* need to die to in your broken relationship?

Burial. This question is humbling, and yet you need to ask yourself, *How will I bury the sinful behavior?* What are your action steps for repentance?

Resurrection. Be free—ask yourself, *What is the newness of life from his Word calling me to do and be?*

Appearance. Allow your life to be changed. How will you show God's transformational work to others in the conflict? How will you demonstrate the fruit of the Holy Spirit in you?

5

≈

Courageous Attitude 1

You Are Controlled by Christ's Love

What or who we worship during conflict will ultimately control us. If we worship a specific outcome and the other person does not worship the same outcome, we will fight about whose outcome wins. If we worship our desires, then our desires will ultimately control us. In his letter, James clearly details this process, talking about how unmet desires that control us lead to sinful behavior (James 4:1–2). In essence, we worship our desires above worshiping Jesus.

We are to have no other gods before God, and that includes our conflict gods (Exod. 20:3; Deut. 5:7). A conflict god might be the god of being right. Or the god of being liked. Or the god of winning. There can be a gamut of different gods we elevate above God, especially when we are in conflict.

We are to worship no other gods beside God (Exod. 20:4; Deut. 5:8). *Worship* is simple to define: giving something or someone our affection, attention, reverence, or adoration. When we worship our conflict gods, we seek others to worship those gods with us. I know I have done it. When others don't worship with us, we break relationship with them. I can give you thousands of examples of how I've worshiped something other than God. That something else then controlled me, and I broke relationship with my spouse, my friends, my congregation, or even complete strangers in favor of worshiping my conflict god.

Instead of allowing ourselves to be controlled by conflict gods, instead of seeking our desires and our outcomes, let's discover what the love of Christ is and how we can allow his love to control us.

The Love of Christ

> For the *love of Christ* controls us, having concluded this, that one died for all, therefore all died. (2 Cor. 5:14)

The love of Christ, first and foremost, is demonstrated by the gospel. As we have already talked about, the gospel is the death, burial, resurrection, and appearance of Jesus (1 Cor. 15:1–8). Jesus gave us the commandment to love, and he declared that there is no greater love than to lay down one's life for a friend (John 15:12–14). *Friend*—that is exactly what Jesus calls you and me. And dying on the cross for his friends is exactly what Jesus did.

However, Christ's love is not only for his friends but also for his enemies: "For if while we were enemies we were reconciled to God through the death of His Son, much more, having been reconciled, we shall be saved by His life" (Rom. 5:10). This always blows my mind. Jesus died for sinners, who are his enemies. That is a tough, brave, and true type of love.

Sometimes our enemy can be the person we are in frustrated conflict with. Here is a tough question: Are you willing to die for your enemy? I know when my flesh gets involved, I am often not willing, nor do I even think of such a concept in the middle of conflict. Paul goes on to state, "*And not only this, but* we also exult in God through our Lord Jesus Christ, through whom we have now received the reconciliation" (v. 11). Not only did Christ die for his enemies, but he died to reconcile them and lift them up into relationship with God. We can have a tough, true type of love that dies to self.

The love of Christ is demonstrated through the gospel by Christ's deliberate laying down of his life for both his friends and his enemies in order to save them and reconcile them in relationship to God. Additionally, the love of Christ is also impossible to separate from us.

> Who will separate us from the love of Christ? Will tribulation, or distress, or persecution, or famine, or nakedness, or peril, or sword? Just as it is written,
>
> > "For Your sake we are being put to death all day long;
> > We were considered as sheep to be slaughtered."
>
> But in all these things we overwhelmingly conquer through Him who loved us. For I am convinced that neither death, nor life, nor angels, nor principalities, nor things present, nor things to come, nor powers, nor height, nor depth, nor any other created thing, will be able to separate us from the love of God, which is in Christ Jesus our Lord. (8:35–39)

Let's break these verses down and evaluate them in terms of your relationship with the love of Christ.

- Will tribulation separate you from the love of Christ? Nope. Go through the most difficult suffering and trials, and Jesus still loves you. When the enemy uses the pressures of life to attack you, he will not win. Christ still loves you. When sin comes knocking at your door, first, don't answer the door, and second, know you are still loved by God.
- Will distress separate you from the love of Christ? Nope. When circumstances cause you to be uncomfortable, Jesus still loves you. When tension and conflict beat you down, you are still loved by Christ. When internal anguish happens, Jesus still loves you.
- Will persecution separate you from the love of Christ? Nope. When your boss is pressing you and persecuting

you, Jesus still loves you. When your children don't want to have anything to do with you, Jesus still loves you. When your spouse is ready to walk out on you, Jesus still loves you.

- Will famine separate you from the love of Christ? Nope. Even if you are starving—physically, spiritually, or emotionally—Christ still loves you.
- Will nakedness separate you from the love of Christ? Nope. It doesn't matter how well you are dressed. It doesn't matter how naked you are. Even when you are completely exposed, Jesus still loves you.
- Will peril separate you from the love of Christ? Nope. When danger comes your way, and when your safety is threatened, Jesus still loves you. You may be led to the slaughter, and Jesus still loves you. You may be put to death, and Jesus still loves you.
- Will death separate you from the love of Christ? Nope. When you die, Jesus still loves you.
- Will life separate you from the love of Christ? Nope. When you have the best day of your life, Jesus still loves you. When you have the worst day of your life, he still loves you. When you have a roller-coaster day, Jesus loves you.
- Will angels separate you from the love of Christ? Nope. A demon can't separate you from God, and neither can one of God's angels. Jesus still loves you.
- Will principalities separate you from the love of Christ? Nope. No dominion in the spiritual realm can separate you from Jesus's love.
- Will things present separate you from the love of Christ? Nope. Nothing here and now on the face of this planet can separate you from the love of Christ.
- Will there be things to come that can separate you from the love of Christ? Nope. Nothing in the future will separate you from the love of Christ.

- Will powers separate you from the love of Christ? Nope. No government authority can separate you from his love. No leader, no person, and no power can separate you from Christ's love.
- Will height separate you from the love of Christ? Nope. Go to the highest height, and you can't be separated from the love of Christ.
- Will depth separate you from the love of Christ? Nope. Dig the deepest hole, or even go into the abyss of the earth, and you won't be separated from the love of Christ.
- Will any created thing separate you from the love of Christ? Nope. Create the most world-changing invention, and still you will not be separated from the love Christ has for you.

There is not one thing, idea, or person able to divide, isolate, or remove you from the love of God, which is in Christ Jesus our Lord. God has decided to love you through his Son, Jesus, no matter what. Therefore, nothing, and I mean *nothing*, can or will separate you from the love Christ has for you. Your struggles, conflict, distress, peril—none of these things can separate you from the love of Christ.

Christ's love—his death and resurrection—causes us to be conquerors. His act of love is overwhelmingly powerful. The inseparable love of Christ surpasses knowledge (Eph. 3:14–19). Consider the most incredible description you can fathom about the love of Christ—Jesus's love still surpasses it. This is powerful. This is wonderful. Jesus's love is amazing. His love will fill you to overflowing.

Controlled by the Love of Christ

For the love of Christ *controls us*, having concluded this, that one died for all, therefore all died. (2 Cor. 5:14)

We are to be controlled by the inseparable love of Christ. Does this include all our relationships? Absolutely! This Scripture is not saying to let the love of Christ control us in our relationship with God but to let selfishness and anger control us in our relationships with others. The Word of God is clear: we are to love God and love others (Matt. 22:36–40). The only way to have this type of love is if Christ's love controls us.

The key to reconciliation is being willing to lay down your life for the other person (John 15:12–14). When you lay down your life for someone else, you are allowing the love of Christ to control you. I am not talking about sweeping issues under the carpet or pretending a negative action has not happened, nor am I talking about avoiding discussion of an injustice or sin. I am talking about having humility and dying to yourself. For some of you, this will mean you need to speak up and tell the truth—taking care to deliver that truth in love. For others, it may be that you will need to be quiet and listen more. The key is to approach any discussion honestly but humbly, authentically but mercifully, and transparently but lovingly.

The love of Christ can control us when we're interacting with our enemy. I know this sounds absurd. You may even say it sounds crazy. However, Jesus's love dwells in you. And God demonstrated this type of love to us (Rom. 5:8). When we were still sinners— enemies—Christ died for us. The question now is, Are we willing to allow this type of love to control us when someone has not repented or when they have not changed?

Romans 5:10 clearly states that "while we were enemies, we were reconciled to God." Let's look at this verse in several translations:

> For if while we were enemies we were reconciled to God by the death of his Son, much more, now that we are reconciled, shall we be saved by his life. (v. 10 ESV)

> If, when we were at our worst, we were put on friendly terms with God by the sacrificial death of his Son, now that we're at our best, just think of how our lives will expand and deepen by means of his resurrection life! (v. 10 Message)

For since our friendship with God was restored by the death of his Son while we were still his enemies, we will certainly be saved through the life of his Son. (v. 10 NLT)

The message in all these versions seems clear to me. We were reconciled while we were enemies of God. Now as Christ-followers we are to imitate Christ—not taking his place but following in his footsteps, his example, his attitude, his love, his walk, his forgiveness, and his reconciliation (John 13:34; 1 Cor. 11:1; Eph. 4:32; Phil. 2:3–8; 1 John 2:6). How are we doing? Do we demonstrate the humility of reconciliation while we are still enemies with our opponent, our adversary, the person we are in conflict with?

When Christ's love is controlling you, you will simply out-love the other person in a conflict. This act of out-loving is so key. It is less based on their response and more based on Jesus's actions. Some of you may protest, "But I am angry with them; they did horrible things to me!" I am truly sorry. And I hope you understand that when you allow the love of Christ to control you, it doesn't mean there will be no accountability for others. It simply means you are relinquishing your right to be the one who holds them accountable and trusting God will hold everyone accountable. The key to walking a reconciled life is to be controlled by the love of Christ, which makes our love for others inseparable.

Look back at Romans 8:35 and take a little quiz to evaluate what is controlling you. Simply check the box that best describes your typical response to conflict.

Conflict	Emotions	Jesus's Love
What primarily controls you during tribulation?	☐	☐
What primarily controls you during distress?	☐	☐
What primarily controls you during persecution?	☐	☐
What primarily controls you during financially tough times?	☐	☐

What primarily controls you during physically tough times?	☐	☐
What primarily controls you during arguments?	☐	☐

For those areas in which you are primarily controlled by your emotions, how do you become controlled by Christ's love instead?

Instead of *controlled*, the King James Version uses a slightly different word:

> For the love of Christ *constraineth* us; because we thus judge, that if one died for all, then were all dead. (2 Cor. 5:14 KJV)

Think of the love of Christ as a fence. This fence *constrains* you, or is the boundary for safety. Christ's love *constrains* you from being lost, hurt, or even relationally killed. Each fencepost is an attribute from 1 Corinthians 13:3–8: being patient, being kind, not being jealous, not acting unbecomingly, not being provoked, not keeping records of wrongdoing, being hopeful, having endurance, and so much more. These attributes are there to support you as you allow the love of Christ to be your hedge of protection. So let patience control you during conflict. Let kindness block you from sinning against the other person. Let hope be a pillar for your relationships. Let humility constrain you. Pray for endurance. Instead of voicing jealousy, proclaim praise. Christ's love dwells in you. Let it flow through you.

Here is the liberating truth: in and of yourself, you will never be able to love others as Christ loves. It is only the gospel working through you that enables you to love in this manner. It is only Jesus's death, burial, resurrection, and appearance in you, through the work of the Holy Spirit, that strengthen you. Demonstrating Christ's love to our enemies requires having an eternal perspective and moving out of the temporal perspective. We are here on earth to glorify God. Now, let's look at the secret to being controlled by the love of Christ.

One Died for All

> For the love of Christ controls us, having concluded this, that *one died for all*, therefore all died. (2 Cor. 5:14)

Are you seeing a recurring theme here? We went in-depth into this in the last chapter by examining Romans 6: the connection of believers to Christ through his death, burial, resurrection, and appearance. The reason I'm emphasizing this over and over is because the gospel is key to reconciliation.

> I have been crucified with Christ; and it is no longer I who live, but Christ lives in me; and the life which I now live in the flesh I live by faith in the Son of God, who loved me and gave Himself up for me. (Gal. 2:20)

Since we are crucified with Christ and are then controlled by or constrained by the life of Christ, we get to live in the love and power that bring glory to the Father.

Go back to Romans 6 and look again at this love that controls the believer. In fact, I double-dog-dare you to read out loud the following ten Peacemaker Proclamations during your quiet time with Jesus. Read each proclamation three times. The Word of God will change your heart if you open yourself to being changed.

Proclamation #1: I do not have to continue in sin because I am controlled by Jesus's love (Rom. 6:1).

You are 100 percent free from sin—not because of your righteousness but because of Jesus's righteousness. That doesn't mean you are not wrestling with your sin nature. The key is you are wrestling and not willfully embracing your sin. Some may read this proclamation and call me a heretic, citing Romans 7, which says we are going to do the things we don't want to do. However, following Romans 7 is Romans 8—which clearly states we are no longer obligated to sin or to live according to our flesh (v. 12).

Romans 8:13 declares that if you are living according to the flesh, you must die. If you are living according to the Spirit, you are putting to death the deeds of the body. I am not saying you won't have moments of sin and wrestling with sin, spiritual attacks, or times in which you stumble. I am saying we can't make excuses for sin simply because we are human. Vertically in Jesus—looking though eternity, looking up—we are 100 percent sinless. Horizontally in Jesus—looking through an earthly lens, looking across—we are sinners saved 100 percent by grace.

Proclamation #2: I will walk in newness of life because I am controlled by Jesus's love (Rom. 6:4).

The same power that resurrected Jesus from the dead dwells in you (8:11). Jesus's resurrection power applies to your conflicts and relationships. This power concept is one of the most difficult things to grasp, especially when you are in the heat of the moment. When I am in a bad mood or an argumentative mood, or have stumbled into the pit of conflict, I can struggle with coming to my senses. Such times are frustrating, and I need to consistently commit to walking in the newness of life provided by Jesus. We must daily set our mind toward a response that glorifies God (v. 6).

Proclamation #3: I am no longer a slave to sin because I am controlled by Jesus's love (Rom. 6:6).

You are not a slave to sin anymore. You don't have to be vengeful. You don't have to be bitter or resentful. You are no longer at the mercy of every thought of anger. You are no longer a prisoner of rage. You are controlled by the patience of Jesus. You are controlled by the kindness of Christ. Today is a new day.

Proclamation #4: I am free from sin because I am controlled by Jesus's love (Rom. 6:7).

You are free. You are free from sin and free to walk in a manner that glorifies God. This is the great outcome of being constrained by the love of Christ. As believers, we do not want to use our freedom as an opportunity to do things that dishonor God (Gal. 5:13; 1 Pet. 2:16).

Proclamation #5: I am alive to God because I am controlled by Jesus's love (Rom. 6:10).

You are alive. No, really: you are truly alive in a bigger sense than anyone who does not follow Christ can ever grasp. This is the part I most want you to understand. Life—now and in the future—is found in Jesus, not in being right. If your hope is in someone or something else, or in a specific outcome, you will be disappointed. However, you are truly alive; therefore, live your life for the glory of God. Live in a way that brings attention to God.

Proclamation #6: I will not let sin reign in my body because I am controlled by Jesus's love (Rom. 6:12).

During conflict, what rules over you? Are you allowing fear to reign? Are you allowing emotions to reign? Maybe it is bitterness? Anger? Not you! You are controlled by the love of Jesus. Jesus's love constrains you from those types of attitudes and reactions. You have Spirit-control over your body and your reactions.

Proclamation #7: I will present my thoughts, emotions, desires, and actions as instruments of righteousness, because I am controlled by Jesus's love (Rom. 6:13).

The music being played out in your life is comprised of amazing notes. You might scoff at me here. "How can he say that? He doesn't know how I have responded." I can say that because I know the Jesus inside of you. Today is a new day, and I want to encourage you to forget the dissonant notes of the past. You are an instrument for God's glory, and the Holy Spirit is the musician. Again, it is not your self-righteousness that makes this possible. It is Jesus's death, burial, resurrection, and appearance in you.

Proclamation #8: I am under grace because I am controlled by Jesus's love (Rom. 6:14).

You are under grace. The key to reconciliation is to understand it is not about laws. Grace is about a relationship with God that flows into our relationships with others. Our relationship with God has to be based on grace or we are in big trouble. What does *grace* mean? "God's grace affects man's sinfulness and not only forgives the repentant sinner but brings joy and thankfulness to him. It changes the individual to a new creature without destroying his individuality."[1] Grace allows the God-envisioned version of you to come out—that version of you God desired and planned out from the beginning of time. You are shaped by the love of Christ through the grace of God.

Proclamation #9: I am obedient from the heart because I am controlled by Jesus's love (Rom. 6:17).

Your heart is engaged in this conflict, and yet you are obedient to God rather than to your fallenness. How? Jesus's love is controlling you. Some protest that they will forgive only when they feel like forgiving. Let me be very clear: feelings follow obedience. Sometimes feelings will never show up. However, as believers we have a bigger vision. We look to our reward in heaven.

> By faith Moses, when he was born, was hidden for three months by his parents, because they saw he was a beautiful child; and they were not afraid of the king's edict. By faith Moses, when he had grown up, refused to be called the son of Pharaoh's daughter, *choosing rather to endure ill-treatment* with the people of God *than to enjoy the passing pleasures of sin*, considering the reproach of Christ greater riches than the treasures of Egypt; *for he was looking to the reward.* (Heb. 11:23–26)

Notice Moses endured ill-treatment instead of seeking passing pleasures. Why? Passing pleasures are, simply, passing. He was looking forward to eternity as his greater desire rather than the temporary things of this life. In conflict, most of the time, we are looking at the temporal instead of the eternal. An eternal perspective will help us to keep focused and to keep an obedient heart toward God.

Proclamation #10: I will present my body as a slave to righteousness because I am controlled by Jesus's love (Rom. 6:19).

You are a slave to righteousness, resulting in sanctification. *Sanctification* simply means to be set apart for God, or holy. God empowers the believer to be holy by the leading of the Holy Spirit. I think sometimes we forget the *Holy* in his name. We could just as easily call him the Sanctifying Spirit. I think we get scared of the word *holy* because in some people's minds it equates to legalism. There is a big difference between manmade rules and God's commands. God's Word will lead you to holiness. Manmade religion will lead you to frustration, comparison, and bondage. In our conflict, we are not looking for a set of rules. We are looking to obey God's Word, thus bringing God glory because we are controlled by the love of Christ.

~~~

I hope these proclamations help you start reconciling your heart with God's heart. Look what the death of Jesus brings for the follower of Christ: death for the believer too—death to sin. While the idea, in and of itself, that we all are dead in Jesus may not sound compelling, after death is the *resurrection*. The resurrection is where things get exciting, especially when we are talking about conflict and reconciliation. Think through this concept: you are freed from sin and empowered to righteousness. I want to yell it. YOU ARE ALIVE! YOU ARE BRAND-NEW! This newness is included in all your interactions with others—and within all conflicts.

LIVING RECONCILED

Practical discoveries that will help you maintain reconciliation:

1. Conflict is inevitable, for we live in a fallen world.
2. Reconciliation is eventual. Seek to have an eternal perspective.
3. You have been given a pledge: you have the Holy Spirit to help you reconcile.

4. The gospel is real. Through the gospel message, you are emboldened to go crazy to glorify God.

5. Let Christ's love—not others—control you.

REVIEW AND RECAP

- What or whom we worship during conflict will ultimately control us. There can be a gamut of different gods we elevate above God, especially when we are in conflict.

- The key to reconciliation is being willing to lay down your life for the other person: you approach any discussion honestly but humbly, authentically but mercifully, transparently but lovingly.

- When Christ's love is controlling you, you will simply out-love the other person in a conflict.

Love is patient, love is kind and is not jealous; love does not brag and is not arrogant, does not act unbecomingly; it does not seek its own, is not provoked, does not take into account a wrong suffered, does not rejoice in unrighteousness, but rejoices with the truth; bears all things, believes all things, hopes all things, endures all things. Love never fails; but if there are gifts of prophecy, they will be done away; if there are tongues, they will cease; if there is knowledge, it will be done away. (1 Cor. 13:4–8)

TO MAKE YOU THINK

Carefully consider each of the following fence posts that support your Christ-controlled love boundary and the question or action that follows. Prayerfully consider your answers and offer them to the Lord as you give yourself up to Christ's control.

- **Patience.** In what areas do you need to be controlled by Christ's love with the natural by-product of patience coming out of your life?
- **Kindness.** How can you be more kind?
- **Rejoicing (not jealousy).** Over what successes of others do you need to rejoice with God and with other people?
- **Praise (not bragging).** In what areas do you need to give authentic praise?
- **Humility (not arrogance).** Ask God to empower you to be humble.
- **Self-control (not acting unbecomingly).** In what areas do you need to exercise self-control?
- **Serving others (not yourself).** How can you practically serve other people—especially those you consider enemies or those you are in conflict with?
- **Temperate (not provoked).** Ask God to forgive you for any times you may have been easily provoked.
- **Forgiving (not taking into account a wrong suffered).** What do you need to forgive and allow God to be the judge of?
- **Faith (believing all things).** In what areas do you need to put your faith in God?
- **Hope.** How can you bring hope into this conflict?
- **Endurance.** What areas and actions do you need to endure in?
- **Unfailing love.** Where has your love failed? Ask God to help you surrender control of those areas of your life to Christ's love.

6

Courageous Attitude 2

You No Longer Live for Yourself

Are you ready to live out one of the greatest practical challenges of being in conflict? What I am about to share with you does not come easily, naturally, or by osmosis. In fact, if you try to achieve it by willpower, it will not work. In conflict, we have a tendency to try to protect ourselves. We will try to shield our reputation or ego; we will spin things to make ourselves look better. This has been evident from the beginning of time; we see it in the creation account and subsequent fall of humanity. When Adam and Eve were asked by God what happened, who did Adam try to blame (Gen. 3:12)? He tried to blame God for his own disobedience, and said his sin was due to "the woman whom You gave to be with me." This blame game is what we do as fallen humans.

In conflict, we have a tendency to focus on the other person's failure. Their injustice toward us will echo so loudly in our ears it deafens us from hearing their statements, their perspective. Think about your most recent conflict. What was the loudest conversation in your head—what was your self-talk? Was it all the things the other person did wrong? Or was it the things you did wrong? Was it all the things the other person could have done better? Or was it all the things you could have done better?

In Matthew 7, Jesus said we will struggle in conflict and will struggle with judging others; other people's contributions to the conflict (or "specks" in their eye) will be easier to see than our contributions (the "log" in our own eye). We must first remove our log—only then will we be able to see clearly to help others. If we want to be 100 percent reconciled and 100 percent at peace, we can't live for ourselves in our present conflict.

Died for All

> *He died for all*, so that they who live might no longer live for themselves, but for Him who died and rose again on their behalf. (2 Cor. 5:15)

It is helpful to look at this verse as a whole. Beginning: Jesus died. Middle: no longer live for yourself. End: Jesus died and rose again.

Jesus "died for all." This statement can be taken a number of different ways, and there is, in fact, a lot of debate over what this means. My primary goal is not to get into a theological analysis but rather to simply look at how Paul uses the word *all* in this portion of Scripture and seek clarity on what he means.

> Through one man sin entered into the world, and death through sin, and so death *spread to all men*, because all sinned. (Rom. 5:12)

Sin entered into the world through Adam and spread to all of the human race and even into creation itself (Rom. 8:19–25). Jesus died for all this sin. As Paul describes the truth of the matter: "for *all have sinned* and fall short of the glory of God" (3:23).

Once again—let's make sure we have this concept firmly in our heads and our hearts—we have all sinned. And yes, that can include how we respond to others when in conflict, be it a simple difference or a multitude of disagreements. I admit it always surprises me when I recognize myself as needing a savior, considering that when it comes to my interactions with others and conflict, I can only see how "right" I am.

> What then? Are we better than they? Not at all; for we have already charged that both Jews and Greeks are all under sin; as it is written,
>
> > "There is none righteous, not even one;
> > There is none who understands,
> > There is none who seeks for God;
> > All have turned aside, together they have become
> >   useless;
> > There is none who does good,
> > There is not even one."
> > "Their throat is an open grave,
> > with their tongues they keep deceiving,"
> > "The poison of asps is under their lips";
> > "Whose mouth is full of cursing and bitterness";
> > "Their feet are swift to shed blood,
> > Destruction and misery are in their paths,
> > And the path of peace they have not known."
> > "There is no fear of God before their eyes." (vv. 9–18)

Jesus is the only one who can take and has taken care of all sin throughout all of humanity—the ugly sin in our lives, in our relationships, and everywhere else. When the Bible says there is none righteous, there really is none who are righteous. We have way more potential to do evil than good, and Jesus died for all of our evil. The Bible describes how our throats are an open grave and our tongues are deceitful, and yet Jesus still died for all of that. Our paths are destruction—and yes, Jesus died for destructive sins as well.

We may think there is a huge divide between the total depravity of humankind, with our need for salvation, and how we act when we are in conflict. I would say there *should* be a huge difference, but oftentimes there is not. The redeemed person should act totally different, but the reality is we do not always experience that difference; I don't always see it in my own life. Jesus died for all the discrepancies between my salvation and my sanctification. Jesus died for all sin in the world, including the sin that has snuck into our relationships.

There is a reason for it. Jesus didn't die just to die.

Death for a Reason

> And He died for all, *so that* they who live might no longer live for themselves, but for Him who died and rose again on their behalf. (2 Cor. 5:15)

Have you ever noticed the number of "so thats" in Scripture? They provide reasons why God tells us to live in a certain way and explain why a previous action was taken. Let's look at a few of these "so thats."

Bible Reference	Truth	So That	Reason
Matthew 7:1	Do not judge	So that	You will not be judged
Mark 11:25	Forgive	So that	God will forgive you
Luke 21:34	Be on guard	So that	Your heart will not be weighed down
John 15:2	Be pruned	So that	You may bear more fruit
Acts 3:19	Repent and return	So that	Your sins may be wiped away and you will be refreshed
Romans 6:6	Let your old self be crucified with Jesus	So that	You would no longer be a slave to sin
1 Corinthians 9:23	Do all things for the sake of the gospel	So that	You may become a partaker of it
2 Corinthians 1:4	God comforts us	So that	We may comfort others

Bible Reference	Truth	So That	Reason
Galatians 3:22	Scripture has shut up everyone under sin	So that	The promise by faith might be given to those who believe
Ephesians 2:10	You are God's work-manship, created in Christ Jesus for good works prepared for us beforehand	So that	You would walk in them
Philippians 2:14–15	Do all things without grumbling or disputing	So that	You prove yourselves to be blameless and innocent
Colossians 1:18	Be filled with the knowl-edge of God's will	So that	You will walk in a man-ner worthy of the Lord
1 Thessalonians 1:6–7	You receive the Word in much tribulation with joy	So that	You become an exam-ple to all believers
2 Thessalonians 1:11–12	We pray for you always	So that	The name of our Lord Jesus will be glorified in you
1 Timothy 5:20	Rebuke in public those who continue in sin	So that	The rest also will be fearful of sinning
2 Timothy 2:4	No soldier in active ser-vice entangles himself in the affairs of everyday life	So that	You may please the one who enlisted you as a soldier
Titus 3:14	Engage in good deeds to meet pressing needs	So that	You will not be unfruitful
Hebrews 10:36	For you have need of endurance	So that	When you have done the will of God, you may receive what was promised
James 1:4	Let endurance have its perfect result	So that	You may be perfect and complete, lacking in nothing
1 Peter 2:2	Long for the pure milk of the Word	So that	By the Word you may grow in respect to salvation

95

Bible Reference	Truth	So That	Reason
2 Peter 1:4	God has granted you his precious and magnificent promises	So that	You may become a partaker of the divine nature
1 John 2:28	Abide in Jesus	So that	When Jesus appears, you may have confidence
Revelation 3:11	The Lord is coming quickly; hold fast what you have	So that	No one will take your crown

This is just a small list of the "so thats" in the Bible. They are all-powerful truths and actions. In our conflicts, we need to live by them. They are the motivators that propel us forward. I know Jesus died for all sin for a reason, and that reason is "*so that* they who live might no longer live for themselves, but for Him who died and rose again on their behalf" (2 Cor. 5:15). Think about this truth in the context of your current relationships. We are reconcilers because we have been reconciled. We reconcile or make peace with others so that God is glorified by our reflecting the gospel to others.

They Who Live

He died for all, so that *they who live* might no longer live for themselves, but for Him who died and rose again on their behalf. (2 Cor. 5:15)

The verse's next phrase, "they who live," is unique and powerful and raises a number of questions. Do some not live? Is everyone alive? Is Paul speaking about physical death here? Spiritual death? If some aren't alive, does that mean they are dead? If we are not alive, can we ever fully reconcile with others?

Let's start with this last idea. In Luke 10:28, Jesus replies to an attorney, saying, "You have answered correctly; Do this and you will live." What was the attorney supposed to do in order to live (or be saved)? The simple answer: love God and love others. Jesus made a clear point of saying those who are truly alive have a healthy relationship with God and healthy relationships with others. In other words, when we love God and live in him, that life affects our relationships with others.

Paul, in mentoring Timothy, explains this relational connection this way:

> It is a trustworthy statement:
>
>> For if we died with Him, we will also live with Him;
>> If we endure, we will also reign with Him;
>> If we deny Him, He also will deny us;
>> If we are faithless, He remains faithful, for He cannot deny Himself. (2 Tim. 2:11–13)

Paul is encouraging Timothy with a biblical truth: "If we die with Him, we will also live with Him." I know I keep making this argument over and over again; however, to be truly reconciled with someone else does not come from "splitting things 50/50" or from getting your justice here on earth. Reconciliation and true life in Jesus only come through the cross. We must die with him to live through him. And only in this attitude can we find the key to reconciliation.

Did you know that Ephesians 2:5 says very clearly that if we are not alive in Jesus, we are dead in our sin? I am not kidding. However, this verse also says that we are made alive together with Jesus by grace. When we have died with Jesus, we can't help being resurrected with him, because we are no longer the ones living. It is now Jesus living in us. Galatians 2:20 makes this abundantly clear. We don't want to go back and rebuild what God has destroyed through Jesus's death. We don't desire to rebuild our sinful nature, sinful responses to others, and our nonglorifying attributes. We are alive. We are new. Because of Jesus.

Therefore, we could rephrase 2 Corinthians 5:15 in this way: Jesus died for all sin so that those who have repented of their sin and laid their life at the cross by grace are alive in Jesus.

Might No Longer Live for Self

> He died for all, so that they who live *might no longer live for themselves*, but for Him who died and rose again on their behalf. (2 Cor. 5:15)

The second courageous attitude necessary for reconciliation is 100 percent based on two facts. First, Jesus died for all of our sins. Second, only those who are alive in him will be able to utilize and maintain the attitude to pursue reconciliation. Just because someone is a Christ-follower doesn't mean they will live out this path to reconciliation; however, all Christ-followers have the opportunity to embrace this attitude.

No longer living for yourself can be a difficult task when you are in conflict. Your body—brain, flesh, heart, and soul—will want to do whatever it can to live for itself. Think about the last conflict you were in. I can almost guarantee part of the conflict was that you were living for yourself. Now consider what intrigues you the most about Jesus. What captivates my curiosity the most is not heaven, Jesus's healing power, nor his provision for us. It is the fact that Jesus died for *my* sin—he did not live for himself.

The selfless acts of the gospel need to resound in every relationship we have. Think how marriages, friendships, and churches would change if one by one we stopped living for ourselves. It is anti-gospel for me to claim to live for Jesus but then live for myself.

For a time, Peter lived for himself. He started following Jesus from a distance and then, when challenged, denied Jesus (Luke 22:54–60). I know it is easy to pick on Peter; he just seemed to place himself in so many contentious situations. Peter had proclaimed he would die with Jesus (Matt. 26:35), yet when faced with the very first obstacle (the first challenge, the first speed bump, the first set of expectations not met), he denied Jesus.

In the midst of conflict, I know I can be exactly like Peter. First, I am willing to result to violence to protect Jesus. Then, when Jesus doesn't respond how I think he should, I get frustrated, and through my actions I deny Jesus. Have you ever done this?

How does Jesus respond to our denial? By calling us to "feed [his] sheep" (John 21:17 NIV). What does that mean? When Jesus says, "Feed my sheep," he isn't saying, "Feed yourself." He is saying, "No longer live for yourself. Feed others!"

What if you looked at conflict as an opportunity to feed others? What if you didn't live for yourself? I know you can't will this change to happen nor muster up enough self-control to do it. None of us can. Fortunately, we don't have to. Jesus has given us everything we need. However, we don't have to just "not" do something—there is an action we are asked to take.

Live for Him

> He died for all, so that they who live might no longer live for themselves, *but for Him who died and rose again on their behalf.* (2 Cor. 5:15)

We get to live for the one who died and rose again on our behalf. Let me say it again: you and I get to live for Jesus, who died for our sins and rose again so that we live in victory today. You are living for the glory of God. You are relating to others for the glory of God. I know you may be thinking, *Uh, no, I'm not. You don't know what I did. You don't know how I responded. You don't know the words that came out of my mouth.* Listen, we have all been there. Repent! Commit to walking in newness of life.

If Peter had sat back and focused on his denial for the rest of his life, he would have been useless for what God had in store for him. Instead, he repented. He spent the rest of his life leading thousands to Jesus (Acts 2:37–47). He preached and was arrested (Acts 3 and 4). Why? He stopped living for himself and started living for Jesus.

Peter still had his issues and relational tension. Paul even had to correct him for his hypocrisy (Gal. 2:11–14). Yet at the end of his life, Peter wrote about "seeing that His divine power has granted to us everything pertaining to life and godliness" (2 Pet. 1:3). God has given you everything you need to glorify him in the midst of your relational tension. You are on a journey to discover more and more of the character of God during your conflict. Don't lose sight of the fact that God is refining you and developing your character.

Here are three actions that will help you live for Christ. They all come from transforming your mind, as Romans 12 tells us: "And do not be conformed to this world, but be transformed by the renewing of your mind, so that you may prove what the will of God is, that which is good and acceptable and perfect" (v. 2).

First, you must present yourself as a living, set-apart, dead thing (12:1). A living dead thing? Yes: you are a living and holy sacrifice. The Holy Spirit dwells in you. You are dead to self and alive to God. You are dead to your temper, your bitterness, your frustration, your selfishness. You are set apart to be an encourager, to be sweet, to bring peace, to be selfless. Why? You are alive in Jesus.

Second, you must prove God's will. When we live for Jesus, who died for us, we prove God's will. God's will is good, acceptable, and perfect. We should not just say on our day of worship how great Jesus is. Throughout the week, we must prove that our worship of God has accomplished something in us (James 2:22–24). It is always a challenge to me in my relationships to prove that God's will is acceptable, perfect, and good.

Third, you must have a humble view (Rom. 12:3). I often have an inflated view of my position, especially when I am in conflict. A humble view relies on the grace that God provides and uses sound judgment. A humble view says, "I might be wrong, and I probably am wrong." Such a view also recognizes we are all created different and see things from different perspectives.

Here is the bottom line of this chapter: Jesus died for the break in your relationship, so no longer live for yourself but live for him.

LIVING RECONCILED

Practical discoveries that will help you maintain reconciliation:

1. Conflict is inevitable, for we live in a fallen world.

2. Reconciliation is eventual. Seek to have an eternal perspective.

3. You have been given a pledge: you have the Holy Spirit to help you reconcile.

4. The gospel is real. Through the gospel message, you are emboldened to go crazy to glorify God.

5. Let Christ's love—not others—control you.

6. You have died, so you no longer live for yourself.

REVIEW AND RECAP

- If you want to be 100 percent reconciled and 100 percent at peace, do not live for yourself in your present conflict.
- No longer living for yourself can be a difficult task when you are in conflict. Your body—brain, flesh, heart, and soul—will want to do whatever it can to live for itself.
- At all times, you are dead to self and alive to God. You prove that your worship of God has changed you. You are humble.

Let love be without hypocrisy. Abhor what is evil; cling to what is good. Be devoted to one another in brotherly love; give preference to one another in honor; not lagging behind in diligence, fervent in spirit, serving the Lord; rejoicing in hope, persevering in tribulation, devoted to prayer, contributing to the needs of the saints, practicing hospitality. Bless those who persecute you; bless and do not curse. Rejoice with those who rejoice, and weep with those who weep. Be of the same mind toward one another; do not be haughty in mind, but associate with the lowly. Do not be wise in your own estimation. Never pay back evil for evil to anyone. Respect what is right in the sight of all men. If possible, so far as it depends on you, be at peace with all men. Never take your own revenge, beloved, but leave room for the wrath of God, for it is written, "Vengeance is Mine, I will repay," says the Lord. But if your enemy is hungry, feed him, and if he is thirsty, give him a drink; for in so doing you will heap burning coals on his head. Do not be overcome by evil, but overcome evil with good. (Rom. 12:9–21)

TO MAKE YOU THINK

In your conflict, what can you cling to that is good?

How can you be devoted to the other person in your conflict?

What practical steps can you take to honor the other person in your conflict?

In your current conflict, what can you pray for?

In your current conflict, how can you show hospitality in a practical manner?

In your current conflict, what practical steps can you take to end paying back evil for evil?

In your current conflict, how can you overcome evil with good?

7

Courageous Attitude 3

You Recognize No One According to the Flesh

Identifying the place and season we are living in is very important. If we think our life and time on earth is heaven, then God will seem unjust. We will constantly be asking, "God, why? Why did that child get hurt? Why did that 'good person' have that terrible thing happen to them?" Recognizing we live in a fallen, imperfect, sinful world brings context to our experiences.

And yet, though this isn't heaven, or even a theocracy, we do know God is involved in our daily lives. We are not in hell. When God created the world, he did not wind up a clock and step away to let it tick away our lives. He is not waiting on the final tock of the clock to dictate when he will step back in. If we look to God's Word, we will see how he is involved in our lives—here and now.

> Do not let your heart be troubled; believe in God, believe also in Me. In My Father's house are many dwelling places; if it were not

103

so, I would have told you; for I go to prepare a place for you. If I go and prepare a place for you, I will come again and receive you to Myself, that where I am, there you may be also. And you know the way where I am going. (John 14:1–4)

Go therefore and make disciples of all the nations, baptizing them in the name of the Father and the Son and the Holy Spirit, teaching them to observe all that I commanded you; and lo, *I am with you always, even to the end of the age.* (Matt. 28:19–20)

Draw near to God and He will draw near to you. Cleanse your hands, you sinners; and purify your hearts, you double-minded. (James 4:8)

In other words, while God is building a place for us in heaven, he is always close by us, here and now, during this time on earth.

So, then, what is Satan's role here on earth? Oftentimes, as believers, we live as if the enemy has no role in our lives. We understand we are not in hell. But Satan does interact with, influence, and corrupt our relationships, our society, and our culture. Again, let's turn to some Scriptures that speak of this conundrum.

And you were dead in your trespasses and sins, in which you formerly walked according to the course of this world, according to the prince of the power of the air, of the spirit that is now working in the sons of disobedience. (Eph. 2:1–2)

We know that we are of God, and that the whole world lies in the power of the evil one. (1 John 5:19)

It is important to note that Satan is a prince, not a king. Jesus Christ is the King of Kings. We struggle with how much God's sovereignty interacts with the authority given to the enemy (Luke 4:6). An interesting picture of these interactions can be seen in Job 1. We know God is good and Satan is evil. Every good gift comes from the heavenly Father (James 1:17). Every evil or bad gift comes from Satan. In other words, the enemy has come to kill, steal, and destroy. Jesus has come to give abundant life (John 10:10).

If this is neither heaven nor hell, what season, time, or place are we living in? I dare to say that we are living in the battle zone, ground zero. Satan is fighting to kill, and Jesus is fighting to give life. That is why Ephesians 6 says very clearly that we need to armor up as if we are in a battle.

> Finally, *be strong* in the Lord and in the *strength of His might*. Put on the *full armor of God*, so that you will be able to stand firm against the schemes of the devil. For *our struggle* is not against flesh and blood, but against the rulers, against the powers, *against the world forces of this darkness*, against the spiritual forces of wickedness in the heavenly places. Therefore, take up the full armor of God, so that you will be able *to resist in the evil day*, and having done everything, to stand firm. Stand firm therefore, having girded your loins with truth, and having put on the breastplate of righteousness, and having shod your feet with the preparation of the gospel of peace; in addition to all, taking up the shield of faith with which you will be able to *extinguish all the flaming arrows of the evil one*. And take the helmet of salvation, and the sword of the Spirit, which is *the word of God*.
>
> With all prayer and petition pray at all times in the Spirit, and with this in view, be on the alert with all perseverance and petition for all the saints, and pray on my behalf, that utterance may be given to me in the opening of my mouth, to make known with boldness the mystery of the gospel, for which I am an ambassador in chains; that in proclaiming it I may speak boldly, as I ought to speak. (Eph. 6:10–20)

We are in a war zone. This time is going to be messy. It is going to be frustrating. It is going to be tough. Let's not shoot our own. Let's not devour each other but rather follow Christ's command to us:

> For the whole Law is fulfilled in one word, in the statement, "You shall love your neighbor as yourself." But if you bite and devour one another, take care that you are not consumed by one another. (Gal. 5:14–15)

That warning leads me back to 2 Corinthians 5 and what actions we can take to live out the calling God has on our lives to be reconcilers. I do have to warn you: our next courageous attitude to reconciliation is challenging to maintain. It is easy to mentally consent to but is another thing altogether to daily apply to our hearts.

Therefore

> *Therefore* from now on we recognize no one according to the flesh; even though we have known Christ according to the flesh, yet now we know Him in this way no longer. (2 Cor. 5:16)

Let's step back and put this verse into the context of what we have been studying. In 2 Corinthians 5:1–10, we discovered that heaven is the believer's destiny or eternal dwelling. We looked closely at acquiring an eternal perspective. In verses 11–21, we saw Paul writing about being reconciled and about Christians being reconcilers. Paul explains that authentic reconciliation can only take place through Jesus Christ. Believers are controlled by Jesus's love, and we no longer live for ourselves. This works

because Jesus died and rose again.
because we have died with Jesus, and Jesus has resurrected us.
because the love of Christ controls us.

From Now On

> Therefore *from now on* we recognize no one according to the flesh; even though we have known Christ according to the flesh, yet now we know Him in this way no longer. (2 Cor. 5:16)

In conflict, and more importantly in reconciliation, we all need a *from now on* experience or moment. This is the courageous step you make when you take control of your heart, your emotions, your thoughts, your desires, and your inner person and say,

"Enough! Yes, what happened wasn't right. Yes, what happened was unjust. Yes, what happened was wrong. But Jesus died for it, and I am going to allow the Word of God to transform my thinking, attitude, and emotions."

As followers of Jesus Christ, we are not by-products of our inner fallenness. We are by-products of the gospel—the death, burial, resurrection, and appearance of Jesus Christ. I like to think of *from now on* as the warrior's stand. Look at King David when he was a young man. David's war cry against Goliath is the same one I think we need to have against our inner fallenness.

> Then David said to the Philistine, "You come to me with a sword, a spear, and a javelin, but I come to you in the name of the LORD of hosts, the God of the armies of Israel, whom you have taunted. This day the LORD will deliver you up into my hands, and I will strike you down and remove your head from you. And I will give the dead bodies of the army of the Philistines this day to the birds of the sky and the wild beasts of the earth, that all the earth may know that there is a God in Israel, and that all this assembly may know that the LORD does not deliver by sword or by spear; for the battle is the LORD's and He will give you into our hands." (1 Sam. 17:45–47)

If we declare the victory of the Lord against our inner selves, living by the gospel rather than the demands of our flesh, we are setting ourselves up mentally, emotionally, and spiritually to handle our conflicts both with others and with our own sinful natures.

In conflict, we often see the other party as being the problem. Yet as we have already identified, the source of our battle is less with the other person and more in the spiritual realm. That is why we need to get to the point where we say to our brains, *Listen, stinkin' thinkin', I've had enough. I'm not going to dwell on my hurt. I'm not going to dwell on my injustice. I'm not going to dwell on how so-and-so treated me poorly. Conflict may be attacking my emotions, but I come at you with the name of the Lord. Conflict may be assaulting me with fear, but God's perfect love is going to cast you out.*

The thing about conflict is it messes with your mind, emotions, and desires—but you are not a victim. Put your foot down and say, "From now on!" *From now on, I'm not going to justify myself; God is my justifier. From now on, I'm not the defender of my life; God is the defender of my life and reputation. From now on, I'm going to be less worried about being right; God is the only one who can take my fallenness and transform it into his righteousness.*

We must have a *from now on* moment if we are going to be able to embrace the next truth from God's Word.

Recognize No One According to the Flesh

> Therefore from now on *we recognize no one according to the flesh*; even though we have known Christ according to the flesh, yet now we know Him in this way no longer. (2 Cor. 5:16)

In conflict, seeing people according to their flesh is the natural way we want to see others. It is easier to see their fallenness, their mistakes, their bad behavior, their anger, and so on. But maybe Paul is not talking about conflict. Maybe I am taking this out of context. Maybe the "we" doesn't actually mean *we*—you and the person you're mad at, or me and the person I'm mad at. Maybe "recognize" doesn't mean identifying with or seeing another person. Maybe "no one" doesn't refer to all other people but really means just some people. God is okay with us negotiating with his Word, right?

The truth is, I really don't like this verse when I am in conflict, because in conflict, all that is screaming at me is the other person's flesh. Their mistakes, their poor choices, their behavior are like a gigantic billboard assuring me, "They were wrong." On the likely assumption that God does expect us to actually obey his Word as it is written, let's look into this verse further.

What is "the flesh"? Well, there are several answers to that question. Paul could simply be talking about our physical bodies: our skin, our hair, our external characteristics. He could be referring to Bible verses that say things like people appraise each other by their outer appearance, but God looks at the heart (see

1 Sam. 16:7). In other words, we should not judge people based on their external characteristics. We should not judge them based on whether they are black, white, brown, or different from us in any other external way. In conflict, we should not regard others according to their flesh.

But what else could Paul be talking about? Viewing others according to a worldly perspective can also be labeled as recognizing others according to "the flesh." In other words, we could view Jesus as simply a good teacher. Or we could see Jesus as the son of Joseph. In other words, humans tend to judge others according to their ancestry, family relationships, or job titles. But in conflict, we should not use the world's judgment of social value or worth.

So, "our flesh" means our external characteristics and our societal place, but it also has internal implications. Nothing good dwells in the flesh (Rom. 7:18). The deeds of the flesh tend to be clearly evident. In other words, we don't really have to guess what the deeds of the flesh are, because they become externally apparent. If you're not sure what types of things are considered fleshly deeds, check out this list from Galatians 5:

> Now the deeds of the flesh are evident, which are: immorality, impurity, sensuality, idolatry, sorcery, enmities, strife, jealousy, outbursts of anger, disputes, dissensions, factions, envying, drunkenness, carousing, and things like these, of which I forewarn you, just as I have forewarned you, that those who practice such things will not inherit the kingdom of God. (vv. 19–21)

Having an attitude that leads to reconciliation means we no longer see or recognize people according to their strife or outbursts of anger. We no longer see them according to their impurity or sensuality.

Now, some may argue, what if the person they are in conflict with has not repented of these deeds? What if they have not turned from their sin? What if they are still intentionally causing dissension and disputes? I hear the frustration. Responding to others in this state is difficult, and it becomes even more difficult when people promise to change and then don't. Let's address this problem by starting with the simplest resolution and moving to more difficult scenarios.

The simplest reconciliation scenario is that all involved in the conflict follow the steps of confession and forgiveness and turn from their fleshly responses to the conflict. At that point, the conflicted people simply start defining each other the way God defines them. They simply remember that they are all children of God and have been bought with the price of Jesus's blood. This is the simple, the best, and should be—and I emphasize *should be*—the most common form of reconciliation.

However, reconciliation typically is not that simple. Usually what happens is a bunch of small blow-ups precede a big conflict, a fight, or sinful behavior. Then people start defining each other according to the flesh. Then people fight and quarrel. They apologize, but somehow the path of the conflict keeps spiraling. One or all of the people in the conflict will keep going back to the flesh or will continue to define the other according to the flesh. This is when it becomes difficult. Without Christ, we humans struggle with holding people accountable and yet not defining them according to the flesh. Especially when we have talked and talked and nothing seems to change.

Oftentimes, we will begin to judge them, telling ourselves they are and always will be that sinful way. They are not trustworthy. They are horrible. We call them names, even if only in our minds. We focus on how evil they are. We think about the injustices in the situation, and how, if we did not have their attitudes or behaviors to deal with, we would be so much better off.

Here is what I know. The longer you set your thoughts on someone else's fallenness, the less likely reconciliation is to happen. I am not talking about sweeping their behaviors under the rug or pretending like the conflict didn't happen. I am referring to recognizing the real break in relationship, taking control of your thinking, and looking at the situation through the perspective of the gospel. It is only through the gospel that we can begin to see the other person's fallenness through a Christ-perspective.

It doesn't mean there is no accountability. It doesn't mean there may not need to be a change in the relationship. It does mean you begin to bring hope into the situation. It does mean you know, no matter what happens, that the gospel—the work Jesus did on the cross—is great enough.

All of this is more about attitude than anything. When we allow the Holy Spirit to shape our attitudes, and we begin to look at the other person through the sacrifice of Jesus instead of assigning motives and playing God, we will respond with his grace. This grace-full response may include accountability and redefining the relationship, but we are truly not playing God. We are assuming the best of the other person.

Prayer is a crucial means to having this perspective. Cry out to God: "Lord, so-and-so is really blowing up at me right now. In this moment, I remember that you died for them. I remember that all of my bad behavior and their behavior are laid at the cross. Help me not to define my brother/sister according to their bad behavior but rather according to the way you see them. Lord, I am frustrated, and all I can see is the injustice done to me. Help me to see that you paid for that injustice. Help me to see they are my brother/sister, and you are our Father."

The clearest way to understand 2 Corinthians 5:16 is by putting it in context of the next verse. While I will be covering verse 17 in more depth in the next chapter, let me say one thing about it now.

> Therefore from now on *we recognize no one according to the flesh*; even though we have known Christ according to the flesh, yet now we know Him in this way no longer. Therefore if anyone is in Christ, *he is a new creature*; the old things passed away; behold, new things have come. (vv. 16–17)

Why would we recognize the other person in the conflict according to the flesh if that is not who they are anymore, because they are brand-new in Christ? Why would we recognize them according to the flesh if the old has passed away? Now, some of you are going to want to argue with that one, but wait until the next chapter before you really start challenging me. For now, I ask you to simply ponder the question, Why would we recognize the other person we are in conflict with according to the flesh if "new things have come" to us all?

We Have Known Jesus According to the Flesh

> Therefore from now on we recognize no one according to the flesh; *even though we have known Christ according to the flesh*, yet now we know Him in this way no longer. (2 Cor. 5:16)

This concept of knowing Jesus "according to the flesh" is amazing. As Paul talks about how we should see each other, he uses the Corinthians' knowledge of Jesus as an example. He says the Corinthians knew Jesus according to his earthly ministry—as a teacher, a good man, and so forth. But the Corinthians probably didn't see him physically. In this simple statement, Paul is compelling the Corinthian church to check their hearts. Is that the only way they know him? Do they recognize only his earthly ministry? He was just a good man?

The real key to understanding this verse is recognizing what happened between Jesus's earthly ministry and his heavenly entrance: the resurrection.

> Jesus said to her, "I am the resurrection and the life; he who believes in Me will live even if he dies, and everyone who lives and believes in Me will never die. Do you believe this?" (John 11:25–26)

It would be foolish, after the resurrection of Jesus, to simply continue to see him as a good teacher, a prophet, a leader, a servant, or a nice man, or from any other minimal, earthly view. Was Jesus a good teacher? Yes. Was he a prophet? Absolutely. Was he a leader? Sure. A servant? Yep! A nice man? Yep. However, he was and is so much more than all of these. He is the resurrection and the life.

He is eternally more than these descriptors. Consider all the "I am" statements Jesus made.

Question: Is Jesus just bread?

Answer: Nope, he is the Bread of Life that takes care of temporal and eternal hunger. Jesus is even the Bread of Life in the midst of your conflict.

Jesus said to them, "*I am the bread of life*; he who comes to Me will not hunger, and he who believes in Me will never thirst." (6:35)

Question: Is Jesus just a light?

Answer: No way! Jesus is the Light of the World. He is the Light of life. We do not have to walk in darkness because of his light. He is the light in the midst of work conflict, home conflict, and any other conflict.

Then Jesus again spoke to them, saying, "*I am the Light of the world*; he who follows Me will not walk in the darkness, but will have the Light of life." (8:12)

Question: Is Jesus just a door?

Answer: No. He is the door—the only door—to salvation. He is also the only door to relational reconciliation.

I am the door; if anyone enters through Me, he will be saved, and will go in and out and find pasture. (10:9)

Question: Is Jesus just a shepherd?

Answer: Jesus is not just any old shepherd—he is the Good Shepherd. He lays down his life for the sheep. He is the shepherd over the fight you had with your spouse, your friend, or your relative.

I am the good shepherd; the good shepherd lays down His life for the sheep. (v. 11)

Question: Is Jesus just one way to have eternal life?

Answer: No. Jesus is the only way—he is the resurrection and the life. He can resurrect your dead relationships. He can bring life to a boring marriage. He is the life.

Jesus said to her, "*I am the resurrection and the life*; he who believes in Me will live even if he dies." (11:25)

Question: Is Jesus another way to God?

Answer: He is the only way. He is the only truth. He is the only life. The only true, lasting reconciliation can happen through the only true way. It is not willpower, it is Jesus.

Jesus said to him, "*I am the way, and the truth, and the life*; no one comes to the Father but through Me." (14:6)

Question: Is Jesus one of many vines?

Answer: No. He is the true vine. He is your source of reconciliation when you stay connected to him.

I am the true vine, and My Father is the vinedresser. (15:1)

Here is my point: if you only know facts about Jesus, if you only know Jesus according to his earthly ministry, and you do not know him according to the Spirit, you will miss out deeply. You will only have a limited view and understanding of who Jesus is. There are so many people in the midst of their conflict who compartmentalize their view of Jesus. They know Bible facts about who Jesus is, but an encounter with him and his resurrection work is missing.

No Longer

Therefore from now on we recognize no one according to the flesh; even though we have known Christ according to the flesh, *yet now we know Him in this way no longer.* (2 Cor. 5:16)

Now we no longer know Jesus *in this way*. Now we no longer know Jesus only from before his crucifixion, death, resurrection, and appearance. We now know Jesus after the resurrection. He is God. He is the Messiah. He is the Redeemer. He is the Savior. We know him as way more than a teacher. He is God crucified and resurrected. He is the conqueror of sin and death.

I would strongly encourage you not to see Jesus as a mere human in your conflict or in any other part of your life. Jesus is God, and he doesn't stop being God just because you are in conflict. He doesn't answer to you. You answer to him. Glorify him in your conflict. Learn to recognize those around you as the new creations they are in Christ Jesus.

LIVING RECONCILED

Practical discoveries that will help you maintain reconciliation:

1. Conflict is inevitable, for we live in a fallen world.
2. Reconciliation is eventual. Seek to have an eternal perspective.
3. You have been given a pledge: you have the Holy Spirit to help you reconcile.
4. The gospel is real. Through the gospel message, you are emboldened to go crazy to glorify God.
5. Let Christ's love—not others—control you.
6. You have died, so you no longer live for yourself.
7. Consider your view; look at people the way God looks at them and not according to their fallenness.

REVIEW AND RECAP

- I am not going to justify myself; God is my justifier. I am not the defender of my life; God is the defender of my life and reputation. I am going to be less worried about being right; God is the only one who can take my fallenness and transform it into his righteousness.
- Therefore, in conflict, we should not regard others according to their flesh. Reconciliation will very likely not happen as long as we set our thoughts on someone else's fallenness.
- This is more about attitude than anything. When we allow the Holy Spirit to shape our attitudes, and we begin to look at the other person through the sacrifice of Jesus instead of assigning motives and playing God, we will give a grace-felt response.

Therefore, my beloved brethren whom I long to see, my joy and crown, in this way stand firm in the Lord, my beloved. I urge Euodia and I urge Syntyche to live in harmony in the Lord. Indeed, true companion, I ask you also to help these women who have shared my struggle in the cause of the gospel, together with Clement also and the rest of my fellow workers, whose names are in the book of life. Rejoice in the Lord always; again I will say, rejoice! Let your gentle spirit be known to all men. The Lord is near. Be anxious for nothing, but in everything by prayer and supplication with thanksgiving let your requests be made known to God. And the peace of God, which surpasses all comprehension, will guard your hearts and your minds in Christ Jesus. Finally, brethren, whatever is *true*, whatever is *honorable*, whatever is *right*, whatever is *pure*, whatever is *lovely*, whatever is of *good repute*, if there is any *excellence* and if anything *worthy of praise, dwell on these things*. The things you have learned and received and heard and seen in me, practice these things, and the God of peace will be with you. (Phil. 4:1–9)

TO MAKE YOU THINK

Read Philippians 4:1–9 about Euodia and Syntyche.

In this passage, Euodia and Syntyche are in need of harmony, and Paul encourages them not to focus on each other's flesh but to set their minds on one another through a redemptive perspective. He tells them to dwell or think on what is true, honorable, right, pure, lovely, of good repute, excellent, and worthy of praise.

Move from *flesh* focus to *eternal* focus.

Write out your view of the person you are in conflict with and then write out God's view. Once you've thought this through, commit to focusing on God's view of the other person and not your own view.

Your view of the other person:

_____

_____

_____

_____

_____

_____

_____

God's view of the other person:

_____

_____

_____

_____

_____

_____

8

≈

Courageous Attitude 4

You See Others as Brand-New

So often in conflict, I find it easy to make excuses for my behavior and begin to think, *If only I had a different set of circumstances, then I would be able to respond to this conflict better.* If my circumstances were different, I would be different. I would be happier. Life would be easier. Certain situations would be less frustrating. But while I don't mean to be rude, I know me and I know a lot about human nature in general, and I don't think this is accurate for most of us.

Here is the reality: two different people can go through similar circumstances and end up with very different results. One will be bitter and one will be empowered. One will be stressed and one will be energized. One will be defeated and one will see opportunity. One will be annoyed and one will be at peace. Why? The secret is "Christ in me."

> I have been crucified with Christ; and it is no longer I who live, but *Christ lives in me*; and the life which I now live in the flesh I live by faith in the Son of God, who loved me and gave Himself up for me. (Gal. 2:20)

Christ lives in you. Christ lives in you even in the tension and the conflict you are experiencing.

Don't get me wrong; when circumstances are tough, just saying, "Christ is in me" doesn't seem to make it easier. But for your soul, for your eternal perspective, I want you to grasp this concept: in the midst of all your circumstances, *Christ lives in you.* The Creator lives in you. The miracle worker lives in you. The Resurrected One lives in you. The Redeemer lives in you. The best friend of all best friends lives in you. God lives in you. This doesn't make you God. This makes you God's possession. You are owned by God. He bought you. He paid the price for you. And he is with you in the midst of your circumstances.

Live by faith in the Son of God. He loves you and gave himself for you. You may not see everything made right at this very moment; however, faith is what we are living. We don't see Christ, but we believe him. We can't touch the Holy Spirit, but we are in his presence and his presence is in us. We may not experience obvious miracles, but we have experienced God moving in our lives. It is faith. Not feelings. So many of us want to say we are saved by faith, but when it comes to our conflict, we don't want to apply faith. We want to apply self-righteousness. We want to apply self-justification. We want to defend ourselves, explain ourselves, and show the world we are vindicated. Yet that is not the faith we live by. In fact, the gospel I know is that I am wrong and a sinner, and Jesus is right and righteous.

If Anyone Is in Christ

> Therefore *if anyone is in Christ*, he is a new creature; the old things passed away; behold, new things have come. (2 Cor. 5:17)

What does it mean to be "in Christ?" I thought Christ was in me. Didn't we just read that in Galatians 2:20? Yes, we did. Here is what is really amazing: Christ is in the believer, and the believer is also in Christ. The togetherness of the relationship is honoring, amazing, and at times too spectacular to even imagine.

However, it may be easy to think about being "in Christ" regarding salvation, but it is another thing to remember being "in Christ" in the midst of conflict. To be clear, I am not saying that we go "in" and "out" of Christ. I firmly believe that believers, Christ-followers, are securely in Jesus Christ. What I am saying is we tend to separate the salvation language from our daily lives. It should not be this way. In a time of peace, I am in Christ and Christ is in me. In a time of war, I am in Christ and Christ is in me. This relationship is not based on works or circumstances but on faith, grace, mercy, and love. I simply wish I could remember this better during my times of conflict.

It can be hard to picture what being in Christ is like, yet we are in other things all the time. When I am in a building, the building hides me. When I have clothes on, my clothes cover me. When I dive into a swimming pool, the water envelops me. When I am in a car, the car encapsulates me. When I was in my mother's womb, her body surrounded me. Christ hides you; he envelops and encapsulates you. He covers you and conceals you. You are "hidden with Christ in God" (Col. 3:3).

The best descriptions I can think of about being in Christ come from the psalms, many of which use language centering around the fact that God is our refuge—even in times of conflict. As Scripture is transformational, let's look closely at Psalm 46, paying special attention to the "thoughs" and what the psalmist says about being in or taking refuge in God. I encourage you to read it out loud. The practice of reading the Scriptures out loud makes us pay more attention to the details and the imagery they produce. They are also declarations of the truth of the Scriptures, and reading aloud helps not just our brains to interact with the words but our hearts and our spirits as well.

Psalm 46

God is our refuge and strength,
A very present help in trouble.
Therefore we will not fear, *though* the earth should
    change

And *though* the mountains slip into the heart of the sea;
Though its waters roar and foam,
Though the mountains quake at its swelling pride. Selah.

There is a river whose streams make glad the city of
    God,
The holy dwelling places of the Most High.
God is in the midst of her, she will not be moved;
God will help her when morning dawns.
The nations made an uproar, the kingdoms tottered;
He raised His voice, the earth melted.
The LORD of hosts is with us;
The God of Jacob is our stronghold. Selah.

Come, behold the works of the LORD,
Who has wrought desolations in the earth.
He makes wars to cease to the end of the earth;
He breaks the bow and cuts the spear in two;
He burns the chariots with fire.
"Cease striving and know that I am God;
I will be exalted among the nations, I will be exalted in the
    earth."
The LORD of hosts is with us;
The God of Jacob is our stronghold. Selah.

No fear—no matter what is going on around us. Why can we have no fear? God is our refuge. When helping people in conflict, I see over and over again that their refuge is in their name, their success, their reputation, or their righteousness. None of that will last long-term. Only God's refuge stands against time and adversity. When you are in Christ, it means you have taken refuge in God. He is your shelter. He is your stronghold. He is with you! Amen!

I know that it may seem impractical to your current conflict to simply say, "I am in Christ." However, if you don't get the Word of God interacting in your heart, you will never get the Word of God flowing in your relationships. God's Word says it so clearly: believers are in Christ and Christ is in every believer.

You are in the Prince of Peace and the Prince of Peace is in you; therefore, you are a peacemaker. Wow! Let me say it again. You are in the Prince of Peace and the Prince of Peace is in you; *therefore*, you are a peacemaker. Peacemaking and reconciliation are the natural by-products of the believer who is in Christ. Reconciliation is not something you conjure up. It comes through having the heart of God in you because you are in the heart of God. God's heart is surrounding your heart.

You are able to surrender to God because you are in Christ Jesus. Humility flows out of you, and your willingness to take responsibility for the injustices you have caused is a powerful demonstration of the gospel that is in you and the gospel that you are in. Think about this. You are standing in the gospel, and the gospel is standing in you. What is the gospel? We already defined it: the death, burial, resurrection, and appearance of Jesus Christ. You are able to reconcile with the other person not based on their willingness to reconcile with you but because you are able to hand all judgment over to God.

A "New Creature," "New Creation," and "New Being"

> Therefore if anyone is in Christ, *he is a new creature*; the old things passed away; behold, new things have come. (2 Cor. 5:17)

What does it mean to be a "new creature?" Well, when we are born, we have a birth date—a physical birthday. When we repent, we accept Jesus into our heart—or maybe more accurately, he accepts us into his, and we are born again (John 3:3). We have a new spiritual birthday, which celebrates the day we are no longer in the kingdom of darkness but have been transferred by Jesus into God's kingdom (Col. 1:13) and have become a new creation of God through Jesus (John 1:13).

Why is becoming this new creation so important? In the middle of conflict, you are going to want to respond in the old-person way. You need to remind your old self that she or he is dead. You need to stand in the authority granted to you by the overcoming work of Jesus to no longer be dictated to by your flesh and instead respond in a God-glorifying way, empowered by the Holy Spirit. Paul reminds us of this God-given authority:

> For if we have become united with Him in the likeness of His death, certainly we shall also be in the likeness of His resurrection, knowing this, that our old self was crucified with Him, in order that our body of sin might be done away with, so that we would no longer be slaves to sin; for he who has died is freed from sin. (Rom. 6:5–7)

You are a new creation because your old self was crucified with Jesus. If you are in Jesus but not new, that would make you nothing. But being nothing is impossible, because being in Christ means a crucifixion of the old self, through faith, that points partially to repentance but mostly to God's grace and mercy. And in God's grace and mercy you are born anew as someone recognized by God.

In the previous chapter we discussed the courageous attitude based on 2 Corinthians 5:16—in which you are not to recognize others according to the flesh. Verse 17 gives us the *why* to that idea: you are a new creature. They are a new creature. You are a new being. They are a new being. If they are brand-new in Christ Jesus, then they are brand-new. So look at them in that way, not according to their outward appearance or social standing.

Not only do the externals not matter but their past patterns of fallenness do not define who they are today. And yet, from your perspective, they may not care. They may not be trying. They may not appear changed or transformed. And for that matter, neither may you. But in Christ Jesus, they are still new. It doesn't matter what their flesh says about them; what does God have to say about them?

Why is it so important to see them how God sees them? Because of how God treats *you*. Have you ever noticed that God's Word rarely calls people out? He seldom dissects people's behaviors only to criticize. God's Word mostly calls people *up*, pointing out behaviors and then directing them to the standard on which they should be focused: his. God's Word challenges people to be more than what they currently are; to believe more, love more, be as Christ more. And while there are times in Scripture when certain individuals are called out, God's Word treats believers as the new creations they are in Christ, directing their behavior upward toward God! We should treat others the same way.

While you can, and often must for the sake of clarity, tell the person you are in conflict with how they have hurt you, at the same time you will present this conversation totally differently depending on how you view them. If you view them as the old creation, you will most likely call them out for their poor choices, labeling and dissecting their behavior to point out their flaws and failures. If you see them as brand-new creations in Christ, you will find your focus changes to calling them to act more as God would have us all act. You are humbly pointing out that God has a better plan.

But here is the most important thing about this: you must first call out your own sin before you can call out their sin. This is challenging. When I am in conflict, I want to think about the other person's fallenness and my own redemption. Instead, I should focus more on my fallenness and Jesus's redemption of the other person. As Jesus himself told us,

> Do not judge so that you will not be judged. For in the way you judge, you will be judged; and by your standard of measure, it will be measured to you. Why do you look at the speck that is in your brother's eye, but do not notice the log that is in your own eye? Or how can you say to your brother, "Let me take the speck out of your eye," and behold, the log is in your own eye? You hypocrite, first take the log out of your own eye, and then you will see clearly to take the speck out of your brother's eye. (Matt. 7:1–5)

Jesus checks our judgments. He is abundantly clear: we should see our own fallenness first and as far bigger or greater than anyone else's fallenness. That is why, when dealing with sin during conflict, we need to look inward and allow the Holy Spirit to search our hearts. As we complete this self-analysis, we want to always remember that if we and they are in Christ, then we are all brand-new.

Living inside of you is the redemptive, transformational power of the Holy Spirit. So often we wrestle with accepting this gift of newness. However, let me remind you to believe what God says about you and shut down what you say about yourself. That anger you feel when you're in conflict does not define you. That depression you feel in response to conflict does not control you. You are brand-new. You are lifted up on the rock of Christ Jesus.

Old Things Passed Away

> Therefore if anyone is in Christ, he is a new creature; *the old things passed away*; behold, new things have come. (2 Cor. 5:17)

When it comes to conflict, I don't think the cliché "water under the bridge" works. "Blood spilt on the cross" is more like it. Jesus's blood paid the price for all of our sin. The old has passed away, and our key to reconciliation is to allow the blood of Christ to pay for all the sin, the hurt, and the injustices we have caused and experienced.

Just as one example, in your marriage, let the old fights pass away. It is time to let go of past hurts and move on. It is time to set your mind on something other than the old. Your spouse is not perfect, but he or she is paid for by Jesus. Jesus died for both of you.

> Not that I have already obtained it or have already become perfect, but I press on so that I may lay hold of that for which also I was laid hold of by Christ Jesus. Brethren, I do not regard myself as having laid hold of it yet; but one thing I do: forgetting what lies behind and reaching forward to what lies ahead, I press on toward the goal for the prize of the upward call of God in Christ Jesus. (Phil. 3:12–14)

We must forget what lies behind. If we are to press on, if we are to reach forward, if we want to be reconciled, then we need to quit focusing on what lies in our past relationships with others. It isn't like Paul is saying to forget what lies behind yourself but to hold on to what lies behind others and become bitter. No! Absolutely not! In our relationships, we must press on toward the prize—the upward call of God in Christ Jesus. It is not at all easy to forgive in this way, but stop gravedigging and start resurrection proclaiming. Put down the shovel and the pick. God has brought us reconciliation and new life through Jesus. The old has passed away.

Bitterness has passed away (Eph. 4:31). Bitterness will never make you better. It is rooted in old, dead stuff. You need to actively let go of any bitterness you are holding on to. Lay it at the cross—daily, if need be. Jesus has already done all the work for you. People argue for their flesh-responses all the time, and the end result is that they live as victims of their flesh. You are not a victim of your flesh. Jesus has conquered your flesh. He has overcome your sinfulness. You don't need willpower to have Holy Spirit power. Holy Spirit power is dwelling in you because you are a Christian.

Renew your mind every day (Rom. 12:3). Take your thoughts captive (2 Cor. 10:5). Don't be controlled by your own thoughts but rather let God's Word control them. Just because you think of something doesn't mean it is true. We all have crazy thoughts. I, for one, have always wondered what it would be like to be a bird. I've had bird thoughts. But I didn't become a bird just because I thought about it. In the same way, your old stuff is gone, dead, and buried. Don't be consumed by your emotions, desires, and thoughts. We all have these experiences. We are humans living in a fallen world. But what God says about you is way more important than what you say about you.

Anger has been conquered in you (Eph. 4:31). Unrighteous, indignant anger that dishonors God is not part of you anymore. Whether it is explosive or internalized anger, God has set you free and is setting you free from it. You can personally do nothing to abolish your anger. You can self-justify it. You can deny it. You can even learn to control it. But you cannot conquer it. Jesus conquered the anger in you and me. Through Jesus, our explosiveness has passed away. Our internal brewing anger is dead because of Jesus. Therefore, we will glorify God.

Slander is also dead (v. 31). Think on this. You do not have to continue to slander the other person in your conflicts anymore. You don't have to talk about their fallenness. You are not here to continually expose others' sins and low times. You can do something great and mighty. You can speak well of others. You don't have to repay evil for evil or insult for insult; you can give a blessing instead (1 Pet. 3:9–14). Why would you do this? Jesus died for you. Jesus died for them too. He made the old pass away, and so it has passed away. He died for all that sin. He paid the price for all that slander.

Are you ready to be challenged? Are you ready to believe what God has to say about you in this process of reconciliation?

New Things Have Come

> Therefore if anyone is in Christ, he is a new creature; the old things passed away; behold, *new things have come.* (2 Cor. 5:17)

"New things have come." This statement generates a whole list of other questions and concerns. *When did these new things come? I don't see new things. And what are these new things?* This is the most difficult part of this verse; however, it is key. Remember 2 Corinthians 5:16, which tells believers to not regard others according to their flesh, their externals, their internals, or their fallenness? This is the *why* to that verse. New things have come. Let me say it one more time, a little louder. NEW THINGS HAVE COME. Hallelujah! We are not trapped by our old perceptions. We are no longer forced to see only from the world's perspective—now we can see according to God himself. Now the only question should be, Who will you believe? Will you believe what your fallen self tells you about yourself? About others? Or will you believe what God has to say about you?

So if "new things have come" is the *why*, let's consider more closely the *when* and the *what*. Scripture says new things "have come." Not "will come." Not "might come." This past-tense—the action has already happened—concept stays true when looking at different translations.

Therefore if any man be in Christ, he is a new creature: old things are passed away; behold, *all things are become new.* (KJV)

Therefore, if anyone is in Christ, he is a new creation. The old has passed away; behold, *the new has come.* (ESV)

Therefore, if anyone is in Christ, the new creation has come: The old has gone, *the new is here!* (NIV)

This means that anyone who belongs to Christ has become a new person. The old life is gone; *a new life has begun!* (NLT)

The new is here and now; it's already happened! Jesus made you new; it is a fact, and the newness process is still happening today. You are brand-new. You can argue with the truth of that statement or simply proclaim it. You can say over and over, "I don't feel new. I don't respond new. I don't live new." And all those things might be true. However, the reality is you *are* new. You can respond new. You can live new. Why? Jesus did all that needed to be done for you to be new. He paid the price for your newness. He overcame all objections to your newness. You are new *now*.

That is the *when* of "new things have come." Now let's focus on *what*, or perhaps more specifically *who* you are in Jesus. While I do know we are in a process of being sanctified, at this time I am emphasizing the newness that has already come. Also, in regard to the person you are in conflict with, something to remember at a minimum is that they are created by God and hopefully are a new creation in Christ Jesus. If they haven't become brand-new yet, that doesn't give you license to sin against them. In fact, it gives you a greater obligation to represent the humble gospel of Jesus Christ to them. With that in mind, here is who you are in all the newness that God provides through Jesus Christ.

You are God's workmanship (Eph. 2:8–10). God's grace is sufficient for this time of conflict. You are saved through faith, and not of yourself. Your life is not about being right. It is not about winning this conflict. It is simply recognizing and living in God's grace over your life. Now, you may be thinking, *Great! I have God's grace, so I do not have to do anything.* That is simply not true. You are his workmanship. God has created you. He has formed you. He has prepared good works for you to walk in. His workmanship is not half-old and half-new. Nor is it half-dead and half-resurrected. His workmanship is 110 percent brand-new, 110 percent resurrected.

You are fruitful (John 15:16). God didn't make you a conflict fruitcake. New things have come because Jesus chose you, and he chose you for this time. It is no coincidence that you are living in this exact time and place. Yes, you may have caused some conflict and generated some tension. However, let me share a little secret with you: God can still turn that conflict around for his good. He has appointed you to come to your senses and bear fruit during this time of tension. He has set this time aside for you to bring glory to him. He desires that you would display your newness of life in Christ through the fruit of the Holy Spirit.

You are salt and light (Matt. 5:13–14). What does salt do? Salt preserves. Salt makes things taste good. Salt cleanses. That is exactly what you need in your conflict today. During your tension, don't lose your saltiness. Bland Christianity is tasteless. You need the saltiness of Jesus to flavor your relationships. You need the humility and kindness of Jesus to flow over your conflict. After all, you are a light in a dark world, and you may be the only light in this conflict. Don't limit your light so that people only see you and your version of rightness and not Jesus and his rightness. You are brand-new. Let that knowledge shine bright. Let humility come and bring clarity to your situation as light brings clarity in darkness.

LIVING RECONCILED

Practical discoveries that will help you maintain reconciliation:

1. Conflict is inevitable, for we live in a fallen world.
2. Reconciliation is eventual. Seek to have an eternal perspective.

3. You have been given a pledge: you have the Holy Spirit to help you reconcile.
4. The gospel is real. Through the gospel message, you are emboldened to go crazy to glorify God.
5. Let Christ's love—not others—control you.
6. You have died, so you no longer live for yourself.
7. Consider your view; look at people the way God looks at them and not according to their fallenness.
8. As Christ is in us, we will see Christ in others too.

REVIEW AND RECAP

- You are in Christ, and Christ is in you. This relationship is not based on works and circumstances but on faith, grace, mercy, and love. Even in times of conflict.
- God's Word says that those in Christ Jesus are brand-new creations. The reason it is so important to see others how *God sees them* is because of how God treats you.
- God's grace is sufficient for this time of conflict. You are saved through faith and not of yourself. Your life is not about being right. It is not about winning this conflict. Simply recognize and live in God's grace.

Do not lie to one another, since you laid aside the old self with its evil practices, and have put on the new self who is being renewed to a true knowledge according to the image of the One who created him—a renewal in which there is no distinction between Greek and Jew, circumcised and uncircumcised, barbarian, Scythian, slave and freeman, but Christ is all, and in all. (Col. 3:9–11)

Don't lie to each other, for you have stripped off your old sinful nature and all its wicked deeds. Put on your new nature, and be renewed as you learn to know your Creator and become like him.

In this new life, it doesn't matter if you are a Jew or a Gentile, circumcised or uncircumcised, barbaric, uncivilized, slave, or free. Christ is all that matters, and he lives in all of us. (vv. 9–11 NLT)

MAKE A LIST

Issues in this conflict I need to lay aside:

_____

_____

_____

_____

_____

_____

_____

_____

_____

_____

Truths I need to put on from God's Word:

9

≋

Courageous Attitude 5

You Have a Ministry

There is a big difference between desiring to be right, justified, or vindicated and having a thirst for reconciliation. There is also a big difference between wanting to control others through disingenuous reconciliation and having a passion for authentic reconciliation. Here is a fact: even when others may not wish to reconcile with you, you can still be reconciled with others. How? Nobody can steal a reconciliation from you that is based not on works but on faith in Jesus.

Let's say you and I are in conflict. How can I have reconciliation that is based neither on my response to you nor your response to me? Imagine with me relationship bank accounts. The monetary value of your offense against me in your account is −$100. Now let's say the value of my offense against you in my account is −$1000. As long as I keep focusing on your bank account and taking note of that $100 you owe me, I will remain unreconciled with you. And you will remain unreconciled with me as long as you keep tally of my $1000 offense against you.

However, let's say you come to your senses and realize that Jesus paid for your $100 and my $1000. And not only did he pay for those offenses, but he deposited an amount into each of our bank accounts equal to whatever Jesus's hypothetical bank account is worth. You then begin to look at me and at yourself through the dollar amount of Jesus's deposit in each of our accounts. And, through that balance, you begin to reconcile our relationship. You reconcile all negatives to what the Jesus bank has to say, and all discrepancies are gone because Jesus took care of them.

Now, let's say I am bitter and won't let go of your or my negative dollar amounts. Does that mean I can devalue your reconciliation that has come through Jesus? Absolutely not. Reconciliation is 100 percent based on what Jesus has done, not what anyone else has done.

You've accepted that reconciliation through Jesus Christ; however, whenever we get together, I continue to act like a jerk to you. What then? Simple: you don't have to stay abused by a bitter, unforgiving, unreconcilable jerk—me—in this situation. You keep praying and asking God how to demonstrate the gospel to me so that I can grasp the reconciliation that only comes through the gospel, and you wait for me to come to my senses. And when I do, then you run and embrace me. And celebrate, as now we have both reconciliation and a reinstatement of relationship. Our bank accounts are balanced and overflowing with reconciliation.

Reconciliation is 100 percent based on Jesus. Reinstatement of a relationship is based on Jesus plus each person in the conflict applying the blood of Jesus to the relationship. Here is the key: you don't need to wait for the other person to reconcile. You can reconcile while they are still your enemy. Why? Because Jesus is the one who truly causes reconciliation.

> For if while we were enemies we were reconciled to God through the death of His Son, much more, having been reconciled, we shall be saved by His life. (Rom. 5:10)

Are you ready for our fifth courageous reconciliation attitude? It will change your heart. This key can be uncomfortable, because it applies to every believer in Jesus. There are no exceptions. There are no different classes in Christianity. An individual can't claim something doesn't apply to them because, well, they don't have this particular ministry, gifting, or ability. God has given all believers the ministry of reconciliation, which is what we will explore in 2 Corinthians 5:18.

Before we dig into verse 18, read verses 18 and 19 together to get the complete sentence. (We will cover verse 19 in more detail next chapter.) Read the following out loud three times:

Now all these things are from God, who reconciled us to Himself through Christ and gave us the ministry of reconciliation, namely, that God was in Christ reconciling the world to Himself, not counting their trespasses against them, and He has committed to us the word of reconciliation. (2 Cor. 5:18–19)

All These Things Are from God

Now all these things are from God, who reconciled us to Himself through Christ and gave us the ministry of reconciliation. (2 Cor. 5:18)

Reconciliation is from God. New creation is from God. The love of Christ is from God. The eternal is from God. It is so important to lay hold of this truth. Salvation is not a human idea. Salvation and reconciliation belong to God. The enemy can't steal them. The world can't drown them out. Your marriage can't undo them. Your kids can't trample them. God has given them to you through his Son, Jesus Christ.

Your newness is not from you. It is not your willpower that will establish it. Some may narrowly argue that this reconciliation is solely and wholly speaking of salvation. However, I would encourage you to consider that isolating the newness God provides through Jesus Christ to only include salvation does a disservice to the two greatest commandments that Jesus proclaimed are the fulfillment of the law.

[He asked Jesus,] "Teacher, which is the great commandment in the Law?" And He said to him, "'You shall love the Lord your God with all your heart, and with all your soul, and with all your mind.' This is the great and foremost commandment. The second is like it, 'You shall love your neighbor as yourself.' On these two commandments depend the whole Law and the Prophets." (Matt. 22:36–40)

The two greatest commandments instruct us to love God and love others. Salvation that belongs to God gives believers the ability to love him with all of our hearts, souls, and minds. It would be an oxymoron to say, "I love God but hate my siblings. I am new toward God, but my oldness is what others get." In fact, John argues this very point.

We love, because He first loved us. If someone says, "I love God," and hates his brother, he is a liar; for the one who does not love his brother whom he has seen, cannot love God whom he has not seen. And this commandment we have from Him, that the one who loves God should love his brother also. (1 John 4:19–21)

John clearly states that the new creation of God's love in us is because God first loved us. He is so bold as to call you a liar if you hate someone else. In other words, to divorce how we respond to our earthly human relationships from how we respond to our heavenly relationship is deceitful. We must come to know God deeper and deeper. His Word doesn't allow us to simply give mental accolades to his new creation in us and then turn around and be whatever we want to in our actions toward others. His Word convicts us. His Holy Spirit overwhelms us to repentance.

Let's look further at what John has to say. Read 1 John 4:7–21 out loud. Read it slowly. Read it multiple times, and while you do, think about your conflict.

Beloved, *let us love one another*, for love is from God; and everyone who loves is born of God and knows God. The one who does not love does not know God, for God is love. By this the love of God was manifested in us, that God has sent His only begotten Son into the world so that we might *live through Him*. In this is love, not that we loved God, but that He loved us and sent His Son to be the propitiation for our sins. Beloved, if God so loved us, *we also ought to love one another*. No one has seen God at any time; if we love one another, *God abides in us*, and His love is perfected in us. By this we know that we *abide in Him* and He in us, because He has given us of His Spirit. We have seen and testify that the Father has sent the Son to be the Savior of the world.

Whoever confesses that Jesus is the Son of God, *God abides in him*, and he in God. We have come to know and have believed the love which God has for us. God is love, and *the one who abides in love abides in God*, and God abides in him. By this, love is perfected with us, so that we may have confidence in the day of judgment; because as He is, so also are we in this world. There is no fear in love; but perfect love casts out fear, because fear involves punishment, and the one who fears is not perfected in love. *We love, because He first loved us*. If someone says, "I love God," and hates his brother, he is a liar; for the one who does not love his brother whom he has seen, cannot love God whom he has not seen. And this commandment we have from Him, that the one who loves God should love his brother also.

When it comes to reconciliation and when it comes to conflict, the same gospel that reconciles us to God reconciles us to each other. The love that abides in us is the same love we demonstrate to others. This love is the "all these things" God speaks of about the new creation he has placed in each believer. It isn't as if believers have one set of love for God and a lesser set of love toward others. Therefore, as we love God, so must we love others, and that brings clarity to "all these things are from God."

Who Reconciled Us

Now all these things are from God, *who reconciled us to Himself* through Christ and gave us the ministry of reconciliation. (2 Cor. 5:18)

God reconciled us to himself. If that idea doesn't make you excited, then you probably don't have a clear understanding of what reconciliation truly is. Reconciliation means that God took our sin and placed it upon himself (1 Pet. 2:24)—he took responsibility. God made our accounts balance. God paid the price through his Son so that justice would be served and his wrath would be curved. That is beautiful. The Creator of the universe, the Maker of all things, the Giver of all life, reconciles us to himself. Wow! Wow! Wow!

God did so in order that we might walk in righteousness. The reconciliation he offers allows us to respond to others much differently than we might have without his gift. I am not expecting the other person to pay for their own sin. Yes, they may need to make restitution for something they stole or broke, or otherwise be responsible for the consequences of their actions, yet at the same time, I understand that Jesus is the one who reconciles all the sin they committed. Jesus is our example and our only hope. We are to imitate Jesus in our conflicts. The gospel is the foundational key to reconciliation. We are to walk in his footsteps. What was Jesus's example? When people tried to tear him down, he didn't tear them down in retaliation. When people threatened him, he didn't threaten them back. When people crucified him, he accepted it and simply died. Why? He knew the Father would resurrect him. He kept entrusting himself to his Father. He knew the Father is a righteous judge.

In the conflict you are in right now, are you returning evil for evil? Are you threatening because you have been threatened? Or are you entrusting yourself to God the Father? He is a good, good God. He is a just judge. He is a righteous advocate. He will bring perfect justice. Can you trust him not to wink at the injustice done toward you? Can you trust him to be fair and honest to you and to the other person?

This kind of trust can be so hard, because when we think of grace and mercy, we often think of God just giving believers a pass in regards to sin. The reality is that God is not okaying sin, nor does he simply ignore sin. Reconciliation means that God withdraws his wrath. We often don't talk about God's wrath, but it is something every believer should take the time to think about, especially when it comes to understanding how great the gift of reconciliation truly is. To help us with our understanding of this aspect of God, here are three New Testament verses. Read through them. Dwell on them. And come to a clearer appreciation of what an unreconciled life means.

> Do not fear those who kill the body but are unable to kill the soul; but rather fear Him who is able to destroy both soul and body in hell. (Matt. 10:28)

> For the wrath of God is revealed from heaven against all ungodliness and unrighteousness of men who suppress the truth in unrighteousness. (Rom. 1:18)

> He who believes in the Son has eternal life; but he who does not obey the Son will not see life, but the wrath of God abides on him. (John 3:36)

God is the ultimate judge. When we try to be the judge, it never works out. And yet many of us often secretly protest that if we entrust our judgment to God, the end result won't be what we want. However, if we are 100 percent honest with ourselves, if we received what we deserved, we would be in trouble as well. It is arrogant to say, "I deserve God's reconciliation, but the other person deserves God's wrath."

Humans tend to love to play judge, juror, and executioner. I know when I am in conflict, I like to do that. However, the reality is I need to recognize the whole truth of the situation: if anyone deserves God's wrath, it is me. If anyone deserves God's punishment, it is me. How dare I look at one of God's forgiven and say, "You don't deserve my forgiveness, let alone God's forgiveness!"

Okay, I will go back to writing and stop preaching. But the truth holds: what we deserve, God has forgiven. So what right do we have to accuse?

In God's courtroom, we see the following individuals. I know this analogy breaks down slightly because the Trinity—the Father,

Son, and the Holy Spirit—are one. However, the general picture still works.

1. One judge: God the Father (Ps. 75:7; John 5:22)
2. One prosecutor: the devil (Rev. 12:10)
3. One defense attorney: Jesus (John 14:16; 1 John 2:1)

Guess who *none* of them are? You! Me! We are not the judge. We are not the prosecutor. We are not the defense attorney. In God's courtroom, there is no such thing as jurors. Where are we? What role do we play? We are in the gallery, watching the gospel unfold before us.

This waiting is what is so hard about conflict and reconciliation. We want our justice now. We want vindication now. We want justification now. We want God's wrath now. However, God has reconciled you and me and every believer through his Son. Although this is beautiful and easy to see when times are good, it is hard to remember when times are tough.

> For it was the Father's good pleasure for all the fullness to dwell in Him, and through Him to reconcile all things to Himself, *having made peace through the blood of His cross*; through Him, I say, whether things on earth or things in heaven. And although you were formerly alienated and hostile in mind, engaged in evil deeds, yet He has now reconciled you in His fleshly body through death, in order to present you before Him holy and blameless and beyond reproach—if indeed you continue in the faith firmly established and steadfast, and not moved away from the hope of the gospel that you have heard, which was proclaimed in all creation under heaven, and of which I, Paul, was made a minister. (Col. 1:19–23)

Reconciliation means that God makes peace with the believer. Peace comes through reconciliation. Reconciliation comes through the blood of Jesus Christ. Period! I know that seems like a hard statement; however, if you invert it and say reconciliation comes through peace, it is not a true statement. The most horrendous act, the most unjust act, was that Jesus's blood was spilt for those who had sin even though he was sinless. He paid for your peace with God and your peace with others.

Through Christ

> Now all these things are from God, who reconciled us to Himself *through Christ* and gave us the ministry of reconciliation. (2 Cor. 5:18)

Reconciliation comes through Jesus. The literal image of the word *through* is to travel in one side and out the other; we walk through a door or a gate. Every time we walk into our homes, we exit the outdoors and enter in through a doorway that opens into a safe environment—just as in Christ, we exit the world and walk through him to enter the safety of the Lord. As Jesus himself said,

> I am the door; if anyone enters through Me, he will be saved, and will go in and out and find pasture. The thief comes only to steal and kill and destroy; I came that they may have life, and have it abundantly. (John 10:9–10)

If allowed, the enemy of your soul will always use conflict to cause havoc in your life: stealing your joy, killing your relationships, and destroying your commitments. True reconciliation only happens through Jesus.

When you travel through this type of reconciliation, you will find green pastures and abundant life on the other side. Going in a different way never works. You didn't pay for the other person's sin. You didn't pay for your own sin. Jesus paid for both. He is the only one who laid down his life for all sin.

Psalm 23, one of the most famous of all psalms, emphasizes this concept of moving through conflict via Christ.

Psalm 23

> The LORD is my shepherd,
> I shall not want.

He makes me lie down in green pastures;
He leads me beside quiet waters.
He restores my soul;
He guides me in the paths of righteousness
For His name's sake.

Even though I walk through the valley of the shadow of
     death,
I fear no evil, for You are with me;
Your rod and Your staff, they comfort me.
You prepare a table before me in the presence of my
     enemies;
You have anointed my head with oil;
My cup overflows.
Surely goodness and lovingkindness will follow me all the
     days of my life,
And I will dwell in the house of the LORD forever.

At different times in our relationships, we will walk through the valley of the shadow of death—not always literal death but definitely relational death. When we walk through that valley, if we stay focused on the table Christ has prepared for us and stay confident in the knowledge that we are walking through—we are surrounded on all sides by—Christ, then through Christ we will see his goodness and lovingkindness following us. Through Jesus, we will dwell more in the house of the Lord than we will dwell in the valley.

We need to understand, however, the visual picture of this valley we will walk through. In conflict, the easy road is typically the wide or broad road. It is easy to slander others. It is easy to blow up. It is easy to threaten. It is easy to go silent. It is easy to avoid. It is easy to become bitter. All these ways are destructive. But the Bible is clear that we are to avoid this easy and wide road.

Enter through the narrow gate; for the gate is wide and the way
is broad that leads to destruction, and there are many who enter
through it. (Matt. 7:13)

Balancing truth in love is the narrow gate we must walk through. Forgiving is the narrow gate. Dwelling on the new things God has done and is doing is the narrow gate. And we can only enter through Jesus, because he is the only gate.

Let's think about all that comes to us through Christ. In times of conflict, it is easy to focus only on what comes through the injustice against us. However, that attitude will never get us anywhere positive. What will move us forward is truly thinking about what comes through Christ. Some of these *throughs* may seem odd at first glance, but take the time to think about them before you pass them off as insignificant or irrelevant.

One, God judges us *through* Jesus Christ (Rom. 2:16). This is essential. If we were to be judged through our own works, we would be in big trouble. In his grace, God looks at our works and judges them based on Jesus's blood. Or, to put it a different way, he looks through Jesus's blood and sees our works. In conflict, we often judge people through their works and through their fallenness—not through Jesus. We must judge others through Christ if we are going to imitate God (Eph. 5:1). Always remember that the same measurement of judgment we place on others will be placed upon us (Matt. 7:1–6).

Two, abundant comfort is available *through* Christ even as we abundantly suffer (2 Cor. 1:5). Now, to be clear, this kind of suffering should not be caused by abundant selfishness, rudeness, or self-induced hardship. The suffering should be for the sake of Christ. However, in conflict, I typically do not suffer for Christ. I suffer for my own ignorance, sinfulness, and sometimes stupidity.

Three, we can be confident when we look *through* Christ toward the Father (3:4). Confidence is not an understatement. Confidence is not an overstatement. Confidence is accessible and given to us through Jesus Christ. We simply can turn to God, knowing that through Christ confidence comes from spending time with Jesus (Acts 4:13).

Remember, we are talking about being reconciled vertically to God and horizontally to others through Jesus Christ. This reconciliation is neither based upon us nor upon them but is entirely based on Jesus. Through Jesus Christ we can have abundant confidence in this type of reconciliation.

> This was in accordance with the eternal purpose which He carried out in Christ Jesus our Lord, *in whom we have boldness and confident access* through faith in Him. Therefore I ask you not to lose heart at my tribulations on your behalf, for they are your glory. (Eph. 3:11–13)

Confidence does not mean we can't remain humble. We are to be confident not in ourselves but in Jesus Christ and the reconciliation that comes through him.

So often, conflict makes me begin to question Jesus's ability to reconcile. Those doubts normally come because I start focusing on the here and now. However, as we discussed previously, if we don't remove the element of time and look to eternity, we forget to focus on the fact that we will be spending eternity with one another, eating together in pleasant relationship.

Gave Us the Ministry

> Now all these things are from God, who reconciled us to Himself through Christ and *gave us the ministry of reconciliation.* (2 Cor. 5:18)

This passage leads to several major questions. Who is "us"? Paul? The Corinthian church? Or does "us" include all Christians—past, present, and future? And what is this ministry of reconciliation about? Does it only apply to salvation and calling people to repentance? Is this ministry of reconciliation absent of daily, practical human interactions? Does a ministry of reconciliation include sharing Jesus with others, and then, once they have been reconciled to God through faith in Jesus, not worrying about living a life of reconciliation? I don't think so. In fact, I know this is not true. Jesus himself told us:

A new commandment I give to you, that you love one another, even as I have loved you, that you also love one another. By this all men will know that you are My disciples, if you have love for one another. (John 13:34–35)

Who is us? All Christians. And what is this ministry of reconciliation about? Always living in love with one another.

When unbelievers see believers reconcile with each other, it draws them to the gospel. In fact, we could liberally rewrite these verses as follows. (For all the Greek scholars out there who are going to read this and then inform me that *agape* does not mean "to reconcile," I understand that. It's okay.)

Reconcile with one another, even as I, Jesus, have reconciled with you, so also you reconcile with one another. By this all people will know that you are my disciples, if you have reconciled with one another.

Reconciliation only comes through the gospel—the death, burial, resurrection, and appearance of Jesus Christ. Jesus laid down his life for all believers. His death is the clearest example of authentic reconciliation. In fact, Jesus said the greatest love we can have is to lay down our life for others (15:13). So, if we take that into consideration, we can rewrite John 13:34–35 yet again:

Lay down your lives for one another, even as I, Jesus, have laid down my life for you, so also you lay down your lives for one another. By this all people will know that you are my disciples, if you lay down your lives for one another.

Every follower of Jesus has the ministry of reconciliation. This ministry is intended both to draw people to the cross and an understanding of the gospel and to be a constant expression that, through our relationships, draws people to God.

And He was saying to them all, "If anyone wishes to come after Me, he must deny himself, and take up his cross daily and follow Me.

For whoever wishes to save his life will lose it, but whoever loses his life for My sake, he is the one who will save it." (Luke 9:23–24)

The ministry of reconciliation is a daily ministry. This is the fifth attitude of courageous reconciliation: we must practice daily living out the ministry of reconciliation. We live daily reconciled to God through Jesus. We must also live daily reconciled to others through Jesus. While the Bible is clear that there are certain ministries God has appointed in the church, and that some in the body will be apostles, some will be prophets, some evangelists, some pastors, and some teachers (Eph. 4:11), God did not limit the ministry of reconciliation to these leaders. He would not want his people to be led by reconcilers while the followers remained non-reconcilers, destructors, and dis-uniters. Okay, so I'm making up words now, but you get my point. To be in ministry is to be a servant. And to serve is to live in reconciliation with others.

A question I like to ask myself is, How can I serve the person I am in conflict with? How can I minister to them? How can I demonstrate the gospel? How do I live in daily reconciliation with them? These are tough questions we must answer if we desire true reconciliation and peace.

LIVING RECONCILED

Practical discoveries that will help you maintain reconciliation:

1. Conflict is inevitable, for we live in a fallen world.
2. Reconciliation is eventual. Seek to have an eternal perspective.
3. You have been given a pledge: you have the Holy Spirit to help you reconcile.
4. The gospel is real. Through the gospel message, you are emboldened to go crazy to glorify God.

5. Let Christ's love—not others—control you.

6. You have died, so you no longer live for yourself.

7. Consider your view; look at people the way God looks at them and not according to their fallenness.

8. As Christ is in us, we will see Christ in others too.

9. All believers have a ministry of reconciliation.

REVIEW AND RECAP

- When it comes to reconciliation and when it comes to conflict, the same gospel that reconciles us to God reconciles us to each other. The love that abides in us is the same love we demonstrate to others.

- What we deserve, God has forgiven. So what right do we have to accuse?

- Every follower of Jesus has the ministry of reconciliation. This ministry is intended both to draw people to the cross and an understanding of the gospel and to be a constant expression that, through our relationships, draws people to God.

You have heard that it was said, "An eye for an eye, and a tooth for a tooth." But I say to you, do not resist an evil person; but whoever slaps you on your right cheek, turn the other to him also. If anyone wants to sue you and take your shirt, let him have your coat also. Whoever forces you to go one mile, go with him two. Give to him who asks of you, and do not turn away from him who wants to borrow from you. You have heard that it was said, "You shall love your neighbor and hate your enemy." But I say to you, love your enemies and pray for those who persecute you, so that you may be sons of your Father who is in heaven; for He causes His sun to rise on the evil and the good, and sends rain on the righteous and the unrighteous. For if you love those who love you, what reward do you have? Do not even the tax collectors do the same? If you greet only your brothers, what more are you doing than others? Do not even the Gentiles do the same? Therefore you are to be perfect, as your heavenly Father is perfect. (Matt. 5:38–48)

TO MAKE YOU THINK

What can you pray for the person you are in conflict with?

What are practical ways you can show love to the person you are in conflict with?

How can you serve or minister to the person you are in conflict with?

How can you demonstrate the gospel to the person you are in conflict with?

10

≈

Courageous Attitude 6
You Have Stopped Counting

If we try, each of us can remember injustices that have been aimed toward us. If we dwell on these injustices, we will end up in a war zone. Ultimately, such war zones culminate in hatred or plotting revenge against someone else. Hate will destroy your life far more thoroughly than it will destroy your opponent's life. To hate is to direct ill will toward another person in words or in conduct. Hate truly is the opposite of love. That is why we see in both the Old and New Testaments clear warnings and commands against hating others.

> You shall not hate your fellow countryman in your heart; you may surely reprove your neighbor, but shall not incur sin because of him. (Lev. 19:17)

> Woe to you when all men speak well of you, for their fathers used to treat the false prophets in the same way. But I say to you who hear, love your enemies, do good to those who hate you, bless those who curse you, pray for those who mistreat you. (Luke 6:26–28)

Hatred can start as revenge or bitterness and then creep into our hearts. We need to be so careful to watch over our hearts, as they are powerful. Their contents flow into all the rest of the areas of our lives (Prov. 4:23). If we are not careful, our hearts can keep track of many offenses. Then, when we come across a similar offense, we will draw from the past—and all previous judgment and prior resentment will flow back into us like a flood of poison. As Martin Luther King Jr. explained the phenomenon,

> Returning hate for hate multiplies hate, adding deeper darkness to a night already devoid of stars. Darkness cannot drive out darkness; only light can do that. Hate cannot drive out hate; only love can do that. Hate multiplies hate, violence multiplies violence, and toughness multiplies toughness in a descending spiral of destruction.[1]

Hate will never help us move forward in reconciliation. We cannot use darkness to drive out darkness. It will all end in the same place of destruction.

The next attitude for reconciliation will be challenging and will take full reliance on the Holy Spirit to accomplish. To review, here are the five attitudes we have studied so far.

Courageous Attitude 1: You are controlled by Christ's love.

Courageous Attitude 2: You no longer live for yourself.

Courageous Attitude 3: You recognize no one according to the flesh.

Courageous Attitude 4: You see others as brand-new.

Courageous Attitude 5: You have a ministry.

The sixth courageous attitude is *you have stopped counting*. Take a deep breath. This is a challenging concept, but do not stop your pursuit of reconciliation. You can truly be reconciled, and ceasing to count is critical to that end. It will take time to master, but you will eventually succeed. How do I know that? I know the Jesus in you. He gives you and me the power of the Holy Spirit to accomplish all he has called us to do—including stopping counting.

Now, as a reminder, 2 Corinthians 5:19 is the second half of a thought started in verse 18, which we explored last chapter.

> Now all these things are from God, who reconciled us to Himself through Christ and gave us the ministry of reconciliation, namely, that God was in Christ reconciling the world to Himself, not counting their trespasses against them, and He has committed to us the word of reconciliation. (2 Cor. 5:18–19)

God Was in Christ Reconciling

> Namely, that *God was in Christ reconciling the world to Himself*, not counting their trespasses against them, and He has committed to us the word of reconciliation. (2 Cor. 5:19)

The most important truth, the priority, is that God was in Christ reconciling the world to himself. "God was in Christ reconciling" is one of the most amazing aspects of the gospel. Let those words sink into your heart and understanding. "God was in Christ reconciling the world to Himself." Reconciling you to himself. He *sought* reconciliation. He *desires* reconciliation.

To truly understand this type of reconciliation, we must first understand a couple of truths about the relationship between the Father and the Son. Jesus said:

> I and the Father are one. (John 10:30)

> Do you not believe that I am in the Father, and the Father is in Me? The words that I say to you I do not speak on My own initiative, but the Father abiding in Me does His works. Believe Me that I am in the Father and the Father is in Me; otherwise believe because of the works themselves. (14:10–11)

The very fact that Jesus and the Father are one is the clarification of this verse. As one, Jesus and the Father work in tandem. As one with the Father, Jesus died on the cross. As one with the Father, he was buried. As one with the Father, Jesus was resurrected. And as one with the Father, he was witnessed. And now Jesus is in heaven—still one with the Father—waiting for the day of his return. Nothing was done by one with any reluctance or even the slightest hesitation from the other because they are one. Jesus is and was part of the Father. And the Father has always been part of—abiding and living with—Jesus.

What is so exciting about this "abiding" is that Jesus says we abide in him and he abides in each believer. Why would he do this? Why would he give up heaven to be on earth and allow us broken, rebellious, conflicted sinners to be one with him? Some of that answer can be found in Jesus's prayer in John 17.

> I do not ask on behalf of these alone, but for those also who believe in Me through their word; *that* they may all be one; even as You, Father, are in Me and I in You, *that* they also may be in Us, *so that* the world may believe that You sent Me. The glory which You have given Me I have given to them, *that* they may be one, just as We are one; I in them and You in Me, *that* they may be perfected in unity, *so that* the world may know that You sent Me, and loved them, even as You have loved Me. Father, I desire *that* they also, whom You have given Me, be with Me where I am, *so that* they may see My glory which You have given Me, for You loved Me before the foundation of the world. O righteous Father, although the world has not known You, yet I have known You; and these have known *that* You sent Me; and I have made Your name known to them, and will make it known, *so that* the love with which You loved Me may be in them, and I in them. (John 17:20–26)

Let me take this list and break it down for you. Look closely at the *that* truths proclaimed, which lead to the desired *so that* outcomes.

That they may all be one (reconciliation).

That they also may be in us (reconciliation).

   So that the world may believe you sent me (reconciliation).

That they may be one (reconciliation).

That they may be perfected in unity (reconciliation).

So *that* the world may know you sent me and loved them (reconciliation).

That they, whom you have given me, be with me where I am (reconciliation).

So *that* they may see my glory, which you have given me (reconciliation).

That these have known you sent me (reconciliation).

So *that* the love with which you loved me may be in them, and I in them (reconciliation).

In other words, Jesus and the Father are one and desire that all believers would be one so that the world would be one: reconciled.

John 17 is vital to understanding what 2 Corinthians 5:19 is saying and is the end of Jesus's longer prayer. In order to fully grasp the impact of the concept of reconciled unity—being one—let's look at the entire prayer. What is so cool about it is that Jesus is praying for you and me! I am going to use *The Message* paraphrase to look at the text, but feel free to read the passage in your own Bible.

Jesus said these things. Then, raising his eyes in prayer, he said:

> Father, it's time.
> Display the bright splendor of your Son
> So the Son in turn may show your bright splendor.
> You put him in charge of everything human
> So he might give real and eternal life to all in his charge.
> And this is the real and eternal life:
> That they know you,
> The one and only true God,
> And Jesus Christ, whom you sent.
> I glorified you on earth
> By completing down to the last detail
> What you assigned me to do.

And now, Father, glorify me with your very own splendor,
The very splendor I had in your presence
Before there was a world.

I spelled out your character in detail
To the men and women you gave me.
They were yours in the first place;
Then you gave them to me,
And they have now done what you said.
They know now, beyond the shadow of a doubt,
That everything you gave me is firsthand from you,
For the message you gave me, I gave them;
And they took it, and were convinced
That I came from you.
They believed that you sent me.
I pray for them.
I'm not praying for the God-rejecting world
But for those you gave me,
For they are yours by right.
Everything mine is yours, and yours mine,
And my life is on display in them.
For I'm no longer going to be visible in the world;
They'll continue in the world
While I return to you.
Holy Father, guard them as they pursue this life
That you conferred as a gift through me,
So they can be one heart and mind
As we are one heart and mind.
As long as I was with them, I guarded them
In the pursuit of the life you gave through me;
I even posted a night watch.
And not one of them got away,
Except for the rebel bent on destruction (the exception
    that proved the rule of Scripture).

Now I'm returning to you.
I'm saying these things in the world's hearing
So my people can experience
My joy completed in them.
I gave them your word;

The godless world hated them because of it,
Because they didn't join the world's ways,
Just as I didn't join the world's ways.
I'm not asking that you take them out of the world
But that you guard them from the Evil One.
They are no more defined by the world
Than I am defined by the world.
Make them holy—consecrated—with the truth;
Your word is consecrating truth.
In the same way that you gave me a mission in the world,
I give them a mission in the world.
I'm consecrating myself for their sakes
So they'll be truth-consecrated in their mission.

I'm praying not only for them
But also for those who will believe in me
Because of them and their witness about me.
The goal is for all of them to become one heart and
    mind—
Just as you, Father, are in me and I in you,
So they might be one heart and mind with us.
Then the world might believe that you, in fact, sent me.
The same glory you gave me, I gave them,
So they'll be as unified and together as we are—
I in them and you in me.
Then they'll be mature in this one-ness,
And give the godless world evidence
That you've sent me and loved them
In the same way you've loved me.

Father, I want those you gave me
To be with me, right where I am,
So they can see my glory, the splendor you gave me,
Having loved me
Long before there ever was a world.
Righteous Father, the world has never known you,
But I have known you, and these disciples know
That you sent me on this mission.
I have made your very being known to them—
Who you are and what you do—

And continue to make it known,
So that your love for me
Might be in them
Exactly as I am in them.

Jesus prays for us. His repeated message and prayer are that we would be mature and of one mind. How does this type of oneness come about? It comes through the Father, who reconciles us to himself through Jesus his Son.

Not Counting Their Trespasses

Namely, that God was in Christ reconciling the world to Himself, *not counting their trespasses against them*, and He has committed to us the word of reconciliation. (2 Cor. 5:19)

Again, attitude six is to stop counting. The Father reconciles us to himself, and then he doesn't count our trespasses against us. Now, if the Creator of the universe can stop counting, so can we. *Stop counting!* If you have ever experienced injustice, this will probably be a difficult attitude to practice. You can't do it in your own power. However, the Holy Spirit dwelling in you will provide reconciliation for you.

Here's an old dad joke for you: a husband and wife are sitting in the pastor's office, getting some biblical counseling. The pastor asks, "What is the problem?"

The husband replies, "When my wife and I get into an argument, she becomes historical."

The pastor says, "Don't you mean hysterical?"

The husband responds, "No, historical. She reminds me of everything I have done wrong for the last fifty years."

I am so glad God doesn't count my trespasses against me. Aren't you glad he doesn't count yours? God declares that for his own sake he does not remember our sin (Isa. 43:25). A logical question to ask is, If God is omniscient or all knowing, how can he not remember something? The fact is he could if he wanted to.

However, he chooses not to remember our sins any longer. He chooses to remember his Son's work on the cross.

You might then logically proclaim, "I am not God. I can't help but think about the injustices I have experienced." And you would be 100 percent correct. If you are a victim of your thinking, you will never be a victor over your circumstances and will never move forward in "not counting."

However, you are not a victim of your thinking.

> For though we walk in the flesh, we do not war according to the flesh, for the weapons of our warfare are not of the flesh, but divinely powerful for the destruction of fortresses. We are destroying speculations and every lofty thing raised up against the knowledge of God, and we are *taking every thought captive* to the obedience of Christ, and we are ready to punish all disobedience, whenever your obedience is complete. (2 Cor. 10:3–6)

> The world is unprincipled. It's dog-eat-dog out there! The world doesn't fight fair. But we don't live or fight our battles that way—never have and never will. The tools of our trade aren't for marketing or manipulation, but they are for demolishing that entire massively corrupt culture. We use our powerful God-tools for smashing warped philosophies, tearing down barriers erected against the truth of God, *fitting every loose thought and emotion and impulse into the structure of life shaped by Christ.* Our tools are ready at hand for clearing the ground of every obstruction and building lives of obedience into maturity. (vv. 3–6 Message)

If you want to live a life that does not count others' injustices against you, there is only one way to succeed. It is not by your willpower. It is not through your own stamina. And it is not done by squeezing the memory, hurt, or offense out of your life. Successfully not counting others' injustices requires entering into warfare of the mind. You must take your thoughts captive.

Let's say I came to your house to harm you. And let's say you were not going to allow me to do so. If you were to take me captive to keep me from harming you, you might tackle me. You might tie me up. You might interrogate me to see why I was there to harm you. You would then call the cops and have me arrested. You would not simply sit there and be a victim and allow me to hurt you and your family.

Bitterness sometimes comes to our house. It tries to attack our thinking. If that happens, tackle that bitterness. Tie it up. Call the one and only cop, Jesus Christ. He will arrest that bitterness and take it to the cross. You are not a victim of your past. You can stop counting. You can let go of all past injustices by laying them at the cross. How? Remember this one fact and root it in your heart: Jesus paid for all injustice. Jesus conquered all sin. Jesus reconciled.

Taking your thoughts captive is key to not counting. Here is what I say to my thoughts when they try to enter into my house: "Nope, we reconciled that injustice, and I am not going to think on it any longer. So-and-so is a child of God. So-and-so and I are 100 percent whole and complete. We are friends because of Jesus."

Now, before you think I'm a nutjob for talking to myself, I would remind you that we all have self-talk. We all have inner conversations going on in our heads about ourselves, others, and circumstances. Self-talk, whether out loud or silent, is how we process and is extremely important. The key to self-talk is determining what we are telling ourselves. Are we going to keep counting and recounting offenses of the past?

Are you going to continue retelling the story of that past injustice that you just don't want to stop counting against the other person?

A beautiful psalm that looks deeply at this concept is Psalm 42. Read it slowly, and as you read, think about what is *the soul* that is referenced in this psalm. Is the soul the Holy Spirit? Or is the soul the psalmist's emotions, desires, or thoughts? Once you've determined that, look again at the psalm and notice what the psalmist says to his soul.

Psalm 42

As the deer longs for streams of water,
so I long for you, O God.

I thirst for God, the living God.
   When can I go and stand before him?
Day and night I have only tears for food,
   while my enemies continually taunt me, saying,
   "Where is this God of yours?"

My heart is breaking
   as I remember how it used to be:
I walked among the crowds of worshipers,
   leading a great procession to the house of God,
singing for joy and giving thanks
   amid the sound of a great celebration!

Why am I discouraged?
   Why is my heart so sad?
I will put my hope in God! I will praise him again—
   my Savior and my God!

Now I am deeply discouraged,
   but I will remember you—
even from distant Mount Hermon, the source of the Jordan,
   from the land of Mount Mizar.
I hear the tumult of the raging seas
   as your waves and surging tides sweep over me.
But each day the LORD pours his unfailing love upon me,
   and through each night I sing his songs,
   praying to God who gives me life.

"O God my rock," I cry,
   "Why have you forgotten me?
Why must I wander around in grief,
   oppressed by my enemies?"
Their taunts break my bones.
   They scoff, "Where is this God of yours?"

Why am I discouraged?
   Why is my heart so sad?
I will put my hope in God!
   I will praise him again—
   my Savior and my God! (NLT)

What did you determine? Let's think through these questions together. If *the soul* is a reference to the Holy Spirit, that would mean the Holy Spirit is in despair. That doesn't make sense, because the Holy Spirit does not despair. In that case, is *the soul* a reference to the psalmists' emotions, thoughts, and desires? *My thoughts are in despair. My desires are in despair. My emotions are in despair.* That all makes sense. So it is fair to say the psalmist is talking about his inner self and not about the Holy Spirit.

Next, we have to ask if the psalmist is a victim to his soul. And the answer is no. In fact, he commands his soul to do something. He is in control of his soul. If you did not read closely, you might have missed this. Look again at verses 5, 6, and 11. Can you find the command?

In verse 5, he commands his soul to place its hope in God. He takes control of his inner self. He takes his inner thoughts—his self-talk—captive. He says, "Listen, buster, you're not in control of me. I am in control of you. You must put your trust or hope in God." He says the same thing in verse 11, and then also commands his soul to praise God. Praise is so much more than singing. It is giving attention to God, and that attention can be through praying, singing, or other actions.

In verse 6, the psalmist talks about remembering God's past provisions. He chooses to focus on what God has done in his life instead of focusing on the appearance of his current circumstances. In other words, he chooses to stop counting failures and start proclaiming God's truth.

Before we move on, let me just encourage you that there is so much more truth and direction in this psalm; read it over and over again. See what else the Lord reveals to you as you study and think about the words.

One final thought about not counting: we can take thoughts captive, and we can command our souls to hope in God. However, if we don't let go of the past, we will be stuck there. If we do not push the past far away from us, we will be like a pig swimming in our own manure—stinking and wallowing in filth. Too graphic? Sorry, I was raised on a farm.

> Let all bitterness and wrath and anger and clamor and slander be put away from you, along with all malice. Be kind to one another, tenderhearted, forgiving one another, as God in Christ forgave you. (Eph. 4:31–32 ESV)

God has reconciled us—paid for our sin—through Jesus his Son. Fight, proclaim against, and put away all bitterness, anger, clamor, and relational manure. God has so much in store for you. Do not allow the past to rob you of his future for you. The enemy doesn't have to get you to be an ax murderer to keep you from being effective for God and his kingdom. All he has to do is convince you to keep counting. If he does that, you will be useless. Remember, the Word tells us, "Submit therefore to God. Resist the devil and he will flee from you" (James 4:7).

He Has Committed to Us the Word of Reconciliation

> Namely, that God was in Christ reconciling the world to Himself, not counting their trespasses against them, and *He has committed to us the word of reconciliation.* (2 Cor. 5:19)

God has committed to us the word of reconciliation. He has committed us to letting others know that Jesus died for them and rose again and that they may have new lives—in short, the gospel message. He has also placed on us the burden to actively demonstrate the gospel in our relationships. He has set us in this word of reconciliation.

As followers of Jesus, we need to be responsible with what has been committed to us. We need to be responsible to demonstrate this type of forgiveness. This type of gospel. Dare I remind you, this type of reconciliation is not based on our works but based on Jesus?

> He predestined us to adoption as sons through Jesus Christ to Himself, according to the kind intention of His will, to the praise of the glory of His grace, which He freely bestowed on us in the Beloved. (Eph. 1:5–6)

God has freely bestowed grace on the believer. He has adopted us. He has predestined us through the kind intentions of his will. Now let us "be imitators of God, as beloved children" (5:1). He has committed us to the word of reconciliation, and we can responsibly have grace that operates through kindness toward those who have wrongly treated us. We can freely bestow grace on others. Why? Because our goal is not to be right and vindicated. Our goal is to demonstrate the gospel.

LIVING RECONCILED

Practical discoveries that will help you maintain reconciliation:

1. Conflict is inevitable, for we live in a fallen world.
2. Reconciliation is eventual. Seek to have an eternal perspective.
3. You have been given a pledge: you have the Holy Spirit to help you reconcile.
4. The gospel is real. Through the gospel message, you are emboldened to go crazy to glorify God.
5. Let Christ's love—not others—control you.
6. You have died, so you no longer live for yourself.
7. Consider your view; look at people the way God looks at them and not according to their fallenness.
8. As Christ is in us, we will see Christ in others too.
9. All believers have a ministry of reconciliation.
10. You have quit counting the faults of others. You have let go of the past.

REVIEW AND RECAP

- We can take thoughts captive. We can command our souls to hope in God. However, if we don't let go of the past, we will be stuck there.
- You must choose to stop counting failures and start proclaiming God's truth.

Among them we too all formerly lived in the lusts of our flesh, indulging the desires of the flesh and of the mind, and were by nature children of wrath, even as the rest. But God, being rich in mercy, because of His great love with which He loved us, even when we were dead in our transgressions, made us alive together with Christ (by grace you have been saved), and raised us up with Him, and seated us with Him in the heavenly places in Christ Jesus, so that in the ages to come He might show the surpassing riches of His grace in kindness toward us in Christ Jesus. For by grace you have been saved through faith; and that not of yourselves, it is the gift of God; not as a result of works, so that no one may boast. (Eph. 2:3–9)

TO MAKE YOU THINK

What are some things you need to stop counting in your current conflict?

How might you demonstrate, to the person you are in conflict with, a non-counting gift based on the gospel?

How might you apply mercy to your not-counting reconciliation?

What role can grace take in your self-talk or internal thinking?

11

Courageous Attitude 7

You Are a Reconciler

Death is real. In fact, every human's day to die is appointed by God, yet many Christians are living as if their relationships simply do not matter. However, for the believer, life is inevitable.

> And inasmuch as it is appointed for men to die once and after this comes judgment. (Heb. 9:27)

Each of your days is written in God's book. God has not destined you to a life of anger and broken relationships. He has set you on a trajectory to demonstrate the gospel. He loves you. He desires the best for you.

> Your eyes have seen my unformed substance;
> And in Your book were all written
> The days that were ordained for me,
> When as yet there was not one of them.

How precious also are Your thoughts to me, O God!
How vast is the sum of them! (Ps. 139:16–17)

God has ordained you for days of reconciliation. He has created you for peace and to be a reconciler. I know reconciliation is not easy. I know it can be hard to comprehend. However, never confuse the fallenness of this world for the perfect plan of God. You are not home yet. You are in this world but not of it. My encouragement to you is when you finally get to go home, be ready to leave without regrets.

We Are Ambassadors

Therefore, *we are ambassadors for Christ*, as though God were making an appeal through us; we beg you on behalf of Christ, be reconciled to God. (2 Cor. 5:20)

We are all called to be ambassadors. What does that mean? According to *Merriam-Webster's Collegiate Dictionary*, an *ambassador* is

1: an official envoy especially: a diplomatic agent of the highest rank accredited to a foreign government or sovereign as the resident representative of his or her own government or sovereign or appointed for a special and often temporary diplomatic assignment
2 a: an authorized representative or messenger
b: an unofficial representative[1]

We are Christ's envoys, representatives, and messengers to the world—his ambassadors. That title has many implications, but rest for a moment in that truth. You are an official diplomat of the highest rank accredited to a foreign country—not a resident of that foreign country but a resident of heavenly assignment. You have been authorized to represent God to the world. This representation extends to both your relationship with God and with others (Luke 10:27).

Wherever you live in this world, whatever country your passport declares, you are not actually a citizen of that country. You are a citizen of God's kingdom.

> So then you are no longer strangers and aliens, but you are fellow citizens with the saints, and are of God's household. (Eph. 2:19)

> For our citizenship is in heaven, from which also we eagerly wait for a Savior, the Lord Jesus Christ; who will transform the body of our humble state into conformity with the body of His glory, by the exertion of the power that He has even to subject all things to Himself. (Phil. 3:20–21)

You are a stranger, an alien, an immigrant, an ambassador in this world. Your citizenship is in heaven.

What does that have to do with relationships, conflict, and being a reconciler? Everything. You will respond differently if you understand you are a representative of God Most High to the person you are in conflict with. In fact, in the context of this Scripture, that is exactly what Paul is speaking about to the Corinthians. We are God's ambassadors. We cannot afford to squander that honor or responsibility.

Yes, you come from Christ, but more importantly, you are an ambassador *in place of* Christ. You belong to Christ, but you are an ambassador *in defense of* Christ. It's a bit like this: my kids are of the Noble family, but they are also ambassadors for the Noble family. Because they carry my last name, when they are speaking, acting, and interacting on my behalf, the *of* is secondary and the *for* becomes of primary importance. Every interaction you have represents the kingdom from which you come. If you have a spicy personality like me, this can seem daunting. But let me tell you something: God creates us all very different, and he is not looking for frozen, boring people who walk around like they just came out of a museum. He is looking for all types to glorify him.

As you are a representative for God, what are some of the characteristics he would have you model for the person you are in conflict with? Here are some ideas to consider.

First, as an ambassador representing God's character, be alert! In order to serve God well, it is important to be aware of the needs of those you are in conflict with. Pay attention to your body language, your words, your attitudes, and your actions. Carry yourself with dignity. You are an ambassador. Even though you may want to glorify God with your actions and reactions, you must be willing to admit that your flesh is weak (Mark 14:38). However, the Holy Spirit dwells in you, and you have the ability to do the right thing. But you must be alert and stay alert to do so.

Second, ambassadors are not rude but serve well by humbly submitting and showing respect to others. *Deference* is not something we like to talk about in today's culture. It is the humble submission and respect God expects of us, and it is critical we handle our conflicts in a way that does not make our brothers, sisters, or enemies stumble (Rom. 14:21). We are to show deference to their needs and emotions. We must not grow fainthearted in doing the right things for God's kingdom.

Third, as ambassadors, we must remember we represent the king and not ourselves. Authentic endurance is a must-have qualification of an ambassador. We cannot give up simply because the battle gets tough. We must show great diligence in order to accomplish God's assignment for our lives. Our response to conflict can be the gospel billboard in someone else's life if we allow God to move through us.

Fourth, ambassadors for God must practice generosity in the area of forgiveness. As an ambassador, you do not own forgiveness. It is not your currency; it is God's currency. Forgiveness owns forgiveness. Therefore, you can generously give it out as an ambassador. You cannot forgive through your own willpower. You can only forgive through the blood of Jesus Christ (Eph. 4:31–32). I often hear those in conflict protest, "I can't forgive!" I simply remind them that this sentiment is 100 percent true—if they leave Jesus out of the equation. Without Jesus, we cannot forgive. However, Jesus has, will, and is the one who paid the price. Therefore, there is no reason to be stingy with our forgiveness. Our lives are overflowing with the forgiveness of Jesus Christ. Share that.

These are just a few characteristics that God would have us—as his ambassadors, his representatives on earth—share with others. Now, let's dive deeper into what God would have of us as ambassadors for Christ.

Making an Appeal through Us

> Therefore, we are ambassadors for Christ, as though *God were making an appeal through us*; we beg you on behalf of Christ, be reconciled to God. (2 Cor. 5:20)

Stop! Did you notice what that verse says? Look again. Don't rush past it. The Scripture says God is using our ambassadorship "as though God were making an appeal through us." God, the Creator of the universe, the Maker of all the human race, the King of Kings, and the Lord of Lords, is making an appeal to others through you. Some might argue that this appeal is only in relation to salvation. I would politely disagree. This appeal is about our salvation and about our relationships with each other. Yes, God desires that we see people reconciled with him. But God also desires that we be reconciled with each other. This I know: if you are reconciled to God, you will be willing to reconcile with others.

Let God's appeal through you be a billboard that declares, "Meekness!" In conflict, this declaration can be very difficult. Anger seems to come out more easily than meekness in most of us. And the more intimate the relationship, the more difficult it can be to show meekness. We can learn so much from Jesus. He is the Lamb of God (John 1:29). He also is the Lion of Judah (Rev. 5:5). This dichotomy is so amazing. He is both the lion and the lamb. The meek and the bold. We are to be Christ-imitators (1 Cor. 11:1), emulating Jesus in his meekness and in his righteous indignation. My problem is, when I am angry, my anger typically comes out in selfish and annoyed indignation. My billboard is advertising,

"Stay away! Run away from me!" Or worse, "You simply do not matter to me." Lord, help me to be meek.

God's appeal through you requires that you be tolerant. Not tolerant of each other's sin or unbiblical behavior, but tolerant of each other's differences. We ought to walk in a way that shows tolerance to different parts of the body of Christ so that we keep working in unity (Eph. 4:1–3). I've worked with and for people who are extremely different from me. They have different skill sets than I do. They have different gifts, views, thoughts, and expectations of excellence. At times, I have failed and have grumbled and complained—thinking my way is better, right, or how it should be done. However, when I have these attitudes, I do not show others that I am tolerant of our differences.

I can almost guarantee that at some point in your current or most recent conflict, you experienced tension because you were trying to be tolerant of a difference or you simply became intolerant of differences. Remember, tolerance does not mean we embrace an actual sin or say that the sin is okay. Tolerance is remembering we are all in process and at a different part of our God-journey. Tolerance is speaking truth but doing so in love.

Does your conflict billboard declare "Self-indulgence!" or does it read "Self-control!"? God is making an appeal through you—is that appeal going to get lost in the messaging of your behavior? There are a lot of areas in our lives in which we need self-control, including our desires, thoughts, and emotions. However, probably the greatest area in which we need to exercise self-control is our words. Controlling our tongues. How we speak of others and to others. Self-control of our tongues is a game-changer.

A great passage about this comes from the book of James. I encourage you to read this Scripture out loud three times. Read it slowly. Pause! Think! Read it again. Reflect. Then read it again.

For we all stumble in many ways. If anyone does not stumble in what he says, he is a perfect man, able to bridle the whole body as well. Now if we put the bits into the horses' mouths so that they will obey us, we direct their entire body as well. Look at the ships also, though they are so great and are driven by strong winds, are still directed by a very small rudder wherever the inclination of the pilot desires. So also the tongue is a small part of the body, and yet it boasts of great things.

See how great a forest is set aflame by such a small fire! And the tongue is a fire, the very world of iniquity; the tongue is set among our members as that which defiles the entire body, and sets on fire the course of our life, and is set on fire by hell. For every species of beasts and birds, of reptiles and creatures of the sea, is tamed and has been tamed by the human race. But no one can tame the tongue; it is a restless evil and full of deadly poison. With it we bless our Lord and Father, and with it we curse men, who have been made in the likeness of God; from the same mouth come both blessing and cursing. My brethren, these things ought not to be this way. Does a fountain send out from the same opening both fresh and bitter water? Can a fig tree, my brethren, produce olives, or a vine produce figs? Nor can salt water produce fresh. (James 3:2–12)

Our tongues can get us in so much trouble. Exercising self-control of them can change our entire lives. We can bless those we are in conflict with or we can curse them. We cannot both be God's ambassador and a destroyer of other people.

But James doesn't stop here. Again, read this passage out loud, slowly. Think about the last verse. Read it again. And read it a third time.

Who among you is wise and understanding? Let him show by his good behavior his deeds in the gentleness of wisdom. But if you have bitter jealousy and selfish ambition in your heart, do not be arrogant and so lie against the truth. This wisdom is not that which comes down from above, but is earthly, natural, demonic. For where jealousy and selfish ambition exist, there is disorder and every evil thing. But the wisdom from above is first pure, then peaceable, gentle, reasonable, full of mercy and good fruits, unwavering, without hypocrisy. And the seed whose fruit is righteousness is sown in peace by those who make peace. (vv. 13–18)

God is making an appeal through you. He wants your fruit to be righteousness. Show your wisdom. Plant the seed of peace and make peace with others.

James goes on to tell us why it is that we fight. Remember, this was originally written as a letter. There is no split from James 3:18 to James 4:1. It is one continuous thought. Read the next three verses out loud. Then go back and reread James 3 and follow them immediately with these verses. Stop and think. Read the passage for a third time.

> What is the source of quarrels and conflicts among you? Is not the source your pleasures that wage war in your members? You lust and do not have; so you commit murder. You are envious and cannot obtain; so you fight and quarrel. You do not have because you do not ask. You ask and do not receive, because you ask with wrong motives, so that you may spend it on your pleasures. (4:1–3)

Unmet desires focused on the wrong things—pleasures of life, selfishness, self-indulgence—will always make your billboard read as something other than the gospel if you do not take control of your tongue, your thoughts, and your emotions. God's appeal is muted when we focus only on our desires, whatever they may be.

Fortunately, James still does not stop his letter at this overwhelming thought. He has a solution to this tongue and self-control issue. Read the next passage (you know it: three times, out loud).

> You adulteresses, do you not know that friendship with the world is hostility toward God? Therefore whoever wishes to be a friend of the world makes himself an enemy of God. Or do you think that the Scripture speaks to no purpose: "He jealously desires the Spirit which He has made to dwell in us"? But He gives a greater grace. Therefore it says, "God is opposed to the proud, but gives grace to the humble." Submit therefore to God. Resist the devil and he will flee from you. Draw near to God and He will draw near to you. Cleanse your hands, you sinners; and purify your hearts, you double-minded. Be miserable and mourn and weep;

let your laughter be turned into mourning and your joy to gloom. Humble yourselves in the presence of the Lord, and He will exalt you. (vv. 4–10)

Here is James's message in bullet points so you can more easily see the thought process in his solution:

* Seek friendship with God.
* Focus on your relationship with and the help provided by the Holy Spirit.
* Give greater grace.
* Be humble before others.
* Submit to God.
* Resist the devil.
* Draw near to God.
* Humble yourself before God.

In short, stop focusing on yourself and focus on God. Focus on the Holy Spirit. Focus on the appeal God is making through you. Ask yourself what you are advertising on your billboard. Then dig in and practice self-control. There is a lot more in these verses. Go hunting for what God wants to show you. And be aware that there are promises in this Scripture passage as well. If you need a new appeal, a new billboard, I would encourage you—challenge you—to get control of your tongue and humble yourself before God.

We Beg You

Therefore, we are ambassadors for Christ, as though God were making an appeal through us; *we beg you on behalf of Christ*, be reconciled to God. (2 Cor. 5:20)

"We beg you." Paul pleads with believers to live differently—to be reconciled and at peace with one another. When we bite and devour each other, we need to be careful not to become consumed by each other (Gal. 5:15). I really like the practical way *The Message* interprets this passage:

> God put the world square with himself through the Messiah, giving the world a fresh start by offering forgiveness of sins. God has given us the task of telling everyone what he is doing. We're Christ's representatives. God uses us to persuade men and women to drop their differences and enter into God's work of making things right between them. We're speaking for Christ himself now: Become friends with God; he's already a friend with you. (2 Cor. 5:19–20)

We cannot live as the world lives. The gospel is too important for us to eat each other alive over our differences. I see, over and over again, in families, in churches, in Christian businesses, and in our communities, factions, disputes, rivalries, and strife (Gal. 5:20). I—along with Paul—beg you to allow Christ to be the center and the focal point of your relationships.

Now, what about the phrase, "on behalf of Christ"? What does that mean? If I ask you to go to the store on my behalf, you would go to the store and get what I need. If you communicate on my behalf, you would speak for me the things I told you to speak. When I was a kid, my brother and sisters and I would sometimes tell each other, "Mom said . . ." At that point, we were speaking on her behalf.

In the Bible, John the Baptist spoke on behalf of Jesus.

> The next day he saw Jesus coming to him and said, "Behold, the Lamb of God who takes away the sin of the world! This is *He on behalf of whom I said*, 'After me comes a Man who has a higher rank than I, for He existed before me.' I did not recognize Him, but so that He might be manifested to Israel, I came baptizing in water." John testified saying, "I have seen the Spirit descending as a dove out of heaven, and He remained upon Him." (John 1:29–32)

Jesus told his followers that he petitions the Father on our behalf.

In that day you will ask in My name, and I do not say to you that I will request of the *Father on your behalf*; for the Father Himself loves you, because you have loved Me and have believed that I came forth from the Father. (16:26–27)

Scripture itself is text written "on behalf of Christ." And what is it that Scripture tells us? On behalf of Christ, be reconciled to God.

Be Reconciled to God

Therefore, we are ambassadors for Christ, as though God were making an appeal through us; we beg you on behalf of Christ, *be reconciled to God*. (2 Cor. 5:20)

Be reconciled to God. When you are reconciled to God, you will be reconciled to others. Remember the bank account of relationship? No one else can deplete your bank account when its reconciler is God through Jesus. Jesus's blood reconciles you with God and with others. Now, you may argue that the other person doesn't want to reconcile with you. It doesn't matter. If you take the offense, if you take the hurt, if you take the injustice, if you take the pain and let Jesus reconcile all of it through his blood, the reconciliation cannot be undone.

The other person may not want to hang out with you. They may not want to be your best friend. They may not want to eat with you. However, you can still be reconciled with them even if they don't want to be reconciled with you. Their account, their debt to you, can be paid for by Jesus in your eyes, whether they want to accept his reconciliation or not. Their attitude in the situation is not the pivotal point. It is your willingness to forgive that matters. Your willingness to let bitterness go. Your willingness to trust that the injustice you experienced or caused can be reconciled by the blood of Jesus because you have entrusted it to him. Nobody can take that reconciliation away from you. You may not have a reinstatement of relationship this side of heaven, but your heart can change to authentic love of your fellow brother or sister in Christ.

I know I am hammering this point in. And I know I have repeated myself again and again. But the power of this sentiment cannot be understated. What are the two greatest commandments? Love God. Love others. How is that even possible? Jesus! Be reconciled to God. And be reconciled to others. How is that even possible? Jesus!

What is the practical, day-to-day expression of that type of love or reconciliation? God's Word, the Holy Spirit, and discernment. The Holy Spirit will direct you through God's Word on how to reconcile with others even if they don't want to reconcile with you.

Even after hearing this, some might argue, "Can't I just love my enemy, the person I am in conflict with, and still not be reconciled with them? I mean, I really don't want to be reconciled with them. I will just love them."

I don't think it is possible to truly love someone and not allow the price Jesus paid on the cross to pay for the reconciliation between the two of you. Why? Reconciliation is not based on you. Reconciliation is not based on the other person. Reconciliation is based on Jesus and the work he did on the cross. What if God said, "I love humankind, but I don't want to be reconciled to them." What if John 3:16 only said, "For God so loved the world" and that was it? We would be missing the gospel. The gospel is not simply about God's statement of love for the human race. The gospel is the active love of God, demonstrated through his Son, Jesus Christ, that reconciled us to himself.

> For God so loved the world, that He gave His only begotten Son, that whoever believes in Him shall not perish, but have eternal life. (John 3:16)

God's love for humankind propelled him to reconcile us to himself by giving his only begotten Son. Think about that again. God so loved the world *that he gave* his only begotten Son. Love that is inactive is not legitimate love. I truly believe that reconciliation between God and me only happens because Jesus paid the price. I also believe that reconciliation between me and any other person, including but not limited to my enemy, only happens because Jesus paid the price, conquering death by resurrecting.

Now, let's dive into a tricky question related to all this: Is forgiveness different than reconciliation? According to Jesus, you (and I) need to

> Be on your guard! If your brother sins, rebuke him; and if he repents, forgive him. And if he sins against you seven times a day, and returns to you seven times, saying, "I repent," forgive him. (Luke 17:3–4)

Forgiveness and reconciliation must be intertwined, but how does that work? To answer that, let's look into the deeper meaning of a few Greek words. In the four Gospels, *aphíemi* is most often used to express forgiveness. Paul uses *charízomai* when he writes about forgiveness, and he uses *katallásso* when he speaks of reconciliation.

- *aphíemi*: "to send. To send forth or away, let go from oneself, to forgive a debt."[2]
- *charízomai*: "grace. To show someone a favor, be kind to, to forgive."[3]
- *katallásso*: "to change. To reconcile. Used of the divine work of redemption denoting that act of redemption insofar as God Himself is concerned by taking upon Himself our sin and becoming an atonement. Thus a relationship of peace with mankind is established which was hitherto prevented by the demands of His justice."[4]

So, forgiveness is extending grace and letting go by canceling a debt. Reconciliation is Jesus paying that debt by taking our sin upon himself and becoming our atonement, and us subsequently changing—becoming new—in him. As we forgive, Jesus pays the price regardless. And as we accept his grace, we are changed into being his ambassadors—his representatives—to others. Therefore, what type of relationship do we have with someone who does not want to reconcile with us or we simply do not want to be around? Well, according to the Scripture, our responsibility is to "If possible, so far as it depends on you, be at peace with all men" (Rom. 12:18).

Be at peace with God, be reconciled to God. Be at peace with others. Be reconciled to others. You can be reconciled with others because of Jesus, even if they do not want to be reconciled with you. You may not have a complete reinstatement of the relationship, but you can give the injustice to God and no longer hold bitterness, anger, resentment, or wrath toward the other person.

LIVING RECONCILED

Practical discoveries that will help you maintain reconciliation:

1. Conflict is inevitable, for we live in a fallen world.
2. Reconciliation is eventual. Seek to have an eternal perspective.
3. You have been given a pledge: you have the Holy Spirit to help you reconcile.
4. The gospel is real. Through the gospel message, you are emboldened to go crazy to glorify God.
5. Let Christ's love—not others—control you.
6. You have died, so you no longer live for yourself.
7. Consider your view; look at people the way God looks at them and not according to their fallenness.
8. As Christ is in us, we will see Christ in others too.
9. All believers have a ministry of reconciliation.
10. You have quit counting the faults of others. You have let go of the past.
11. God created you to be a reconciler, an ambassador for Christ.

REVIEW AND RECAP

- You will respond differently to conflict if you understand you are a representative of God Most High to the person you are in conflict with.
- Probably the greatest area in which we need to exercise self-control is our words. How we speak of and to others. Self-control of our tongues is a game-changer.
- You can still be reconciled if the person you're in conflict with doesn't want to be reconciled with you. Their attitude in the situation is not the pivotal point. It is your willingness to forgive that matters.

In Psalm 51, King David repents of his sin. He desires to be authentically reconciled with God. Even though he had sinned against Bathsheba by committing adultery and against her husband by having him killed, David understood that ultimately all of his sin was against God. You can read part of his story in 2 Samuel 11 and 12. Carefully read his words in this psalm, and notice how his reconciliation focus is first with God.

Psalm 51

Be gracious to me, O God, according to Your
   lovingkindness;
According to the greatness of Your compassion blot out
   my transgressions.
Wash me thoroughly from my iniquity
And cleanse me from my sin.
For I know my transgressions,
And my sin is ever before me.
Against You, You only, I have sinned
And done what is evil in Your sight,
So that You are justified when You speak
And blameless when You judge.

Behold, I was brought forth in iniquity,
And in sin my mother conceived me.

Behold, You desire truth in the innermost being,
And in the hidden part You will make me know wisdom.
Purify me with hyssop, and I shall be clean;
Wash me, and I shall be whiter than snow.
Make me to hear joy and gladness,
Let the bones which You have broken rejoice.
Hide Your face from my sins
And blot out all my iniquities.

Create in me a clean heart, O God,
And renew a steadfast spirit within me.
Do not cast me away from Your presence
And do not take Your Holy Spirit from me.
Restore to me the joy of Your salvation
And sustain me with a willing spirit.
Then I will teach transgressors Your ways,
And sinners will be converted to You.

Deliver me from blood guiltiness, O God, the God of my
    salvation;
Then my tongue will joyfully sing of Your
    righteousness.
O Lord, open my lips,
That my mouth may declare Your praise.
For You do not delight in sacrifice, otherwise I would give
    it;
You are not pleased with burnt offering.
The sacrifices of God are a broken spirit;
A broken and a contrite heart, O God, You will not
    despise.

By Your favor do good to Zion;
Build the walls of Jerusalem.
Then You will delight in righteous sacrifices,
In burnt offering and whole burnt offering;
Then young bulls will be offered on Your altar.

TO MAKE YOU THINK

In what areas do you need to receive God's grace?

In what areas do you need God to reconcile you through his Son?

How have you sinned against others?

What needs to be cleaned up in your heart?

Do you need to experience the joy of God's salvation again? Explain.

12

At Your Greatest Point of Injustice

Look down at your feet. What are you wearing? Boots? Tennis shoes? Socks? Slippers? Flip flops? Are you barefoot? Do you have hairy feet? Polished toenails? Do you have an ingrown toenail? High arches? Flat feet? Fat toes? Skinny toes? Aching feet? What are your feet doing this very moment? Maybe you have a broken foot. Maybe you don't have feet. Or maybe your feet don't work. No matter what your situation is, Jesus walked in your shoes. He understands what you are going through. He understands every temptation, every struggle, every frustration, and every ounce of your own sinfulness. Jesus relates to our weaknesses. He has been tempted in all things.

> Therefore, since we have a great high priest who has passed through the heavens, Jesus the Son of God, let us hold fast our confession. For we do not have a high priest who cannot sympathize with our weaknesses, but One who has been tempted in all things as we are, yet without sin. Therefore let us draw near with confidence to the

throne of grace, so that we may receive mercy and find grace to help in time of need. (Heb. 4:14–16)

And Jesus has done more than just walk in your shoes. He died in your place. He is the solution to your reconciliation. He is the payment for your reconciliation. And he is the only one who can bring reconciliation. Run to him. Draw near to him, and you will find grace and mercy. He understands more than you will ever know.

Sometimes we think that Jesus doesn't fully understand what we are going through. Let's look at Psalm 139, an encouraging psalm that shows he really does understand. Read it three times, out loud. As you read, contemplate God's intimate knowledge and understanding of you, and after you've read it the third time, focus your attention specifically on verses 23 and 24.

Psalm 139

O LORD, You have searched me and known me.
You know when I sit down and when I rise up;
You understand my thought from afar.
You scrutinize my path and my lying down,
And are intimately acquainted with all my ways.
Even before there is a word on my tongue,
Behold, O LORD, You know it all.
You have enclosed me behind and before,
And laid Your hand upon me.
Such knowledge is too wonderful for me;
It is too high, I cannot attain to it.

Where can I go from Your Spirit?
Or where can I flee from Your presence?
If I ascend to heaven, You are there;
If I make my bed in Sheol, behold, You are there.
If I take the wings of the dawn,
If I dwell in the remotest part of the sea,
Even there Your hand will lead me,
And Your right hand will lay hold of me.
If I say, "Surely the darkness will overwhelm me,

And the light around me will be night,"
Even the darkness is not dark to You,
And the night is as bright as the day.
Darkness and light are alike to You.

For You formed my inward parts;
You wove me in my mother's womb.
I will give thanks to You, for I am fearfully and
    wonderfully made;
Wonderful are Your works,
And my soul knows it very well.
My frame was not hidden from You,
When I was made in secret,
And skillfully wrought in the depths of the earth;
Your eyes have seen my unformed substance;
And in Your book were all written
The days that were ordained for me,
When as yet there was not one of them.

How precious also are Your thoughts to me, O God!
How vast is the sum of them!
If I should count them, they would outnumber the sand.
When I awake, I am still with You.

O that You would slay the wicked, O God;
Depart from me, therefore, men of bloodshed.
For they speak against You wickedly,
And Your enemies take Your name in vain.
Do I not hate those who hate You, O Lord?
And do I not loathe those who rise up against You?
I hate them with the utmost hatred;
They have become my enemies.

Search me, O God, and know my heart;
Try me and know my anxious thoughts;
And see if there be any hurtful way in me,
And lead me in the everlasting way.

As you look at the injustices of this world and the injustices in
your life, I want you to think about this fact: Jesus understands

you. Jesus understands the people you're in conflict with. In fact, the cross is the greatest point of injustice and yet is also the greatest point of justice.

He Made Him Who Knew No Sin

> *He made Him who knew no sin* to be sin on our behalf, so that we might become the righteousness of God in Him. (2 Cor. 5:21)

Jesus was, is, and has always been 100 percent sinless. He is fully God and yet fully human. It blows my mind that Jesus humbled himself and became a baby, taking on the likeness of sinful flesh (Rom. 8:3–4). Physically, Jesus did not come from the seed of Joseph but from the Holy Spirit. The sinful seed of Adam was removed from the equation. The holy child, Jesus, is the Son of God (Luke 1:35). We could discuss in great depth the virgin birth, but that is not the point of this book. Here is an overly simple summary: through Mary, Jesus is fully human, and through the Holy Spirit, Jesus is fully God. Without Adam, Jesus is fully righteous. And Jesus is eternal. Figure out the depth of meaning in all those mind-boggling facts, if you can. For our purposes, let's focus on Jesus's sinlessness.

Being sinless means Jesus is holy. Scripture often talks about God's holiness while simultaneously stating that we, Christ's followers, should be holy as well.

> Speak to all the congregation of the sons of Israel and say to them, "You shall be holy, for I the LORD your God am holy." (Lev. 19:2)

> As obedient children, do not be conformed to the former lusts which were yours in your ignorance, but like the Holy One who called you, be holy yourselves also in all your behavior; because it is written, "You shall be holy, for I am holy." (1 Pet. 1:14–16)

These are just two of the numerous Scriptures that encourage and command us, as followers of Christ, to allow the Holy Spirit to transform us. This is important because it means we can't simply say, "Well, I am human, and therefore, I have an excuse to sin and to not reconcile." No! We are to follow in Christ's footsteps—his character, his likeness. We should make no excuses for our flesh.

What does being holy mean? Being holy simply means being devoted to God's service and abstaining from the fleshly things of this world. Jesus was not a by-product of his human tent. Likewise, we are not by-products of our human tents—our emotions, desires, fears, thoughts, anger, or any other part of our humanity. In Christ Jesus and through the power of the Holy Spirit, we are and can be holy as Christ is holy.

Jesus is pure. He is the Lamb of God. Have you ever seen a lamb? They are cute and adorable. They *look* pure and innocent—but Jesus *is* pure and innocent.

> Beloved, now we are children of God, and it has not appeared as yet what we will be. We know that when He appears, we will be like Him, because we will see Him just as He is. And everyone who has this hope fixed on Him purifies himself, just as He is pure. Everyone who practices sin also practices lawlessness; and sin is lawlessness. You know that He appeared in order to take away sins; and in Him there is no sin. (1 John 3:2–5)

I love this passage because it balances our present state with our future state. For example, "It has not appeared as yet what we will be" but we know "we will be like Him" (v. 2). Do we give up because we are not already pure like he is pure? Absolutely not. Our present objective is to fix our hope on him, for when we do, the Holy Spirit continually purifies us. "And everyone who has this hope *fixed* on Him purifies himself, just as He is pure" (v. 3). Our future hope dictates our current state.

Some might argue that purity is easy when someone is at church on Sunday but not so easy when they are at odds or in conflict with another person, or even simply frustrated with someone else. I understand. At the same time, there is no exception clause. The Bible doesn't say, "Be impure in your conflict and pure in your worship at church." Nor does it say, "When you are mad, it is okay to have impure, evil thoughts, but when you are happy, be pure." Our circumstances do not change what God expects of us.

We are purified by fixing our hope on Jesus, and not only partially pure; we are just as pure as Christ. Why? Because our purity is not based on us but on him who purifies. Jesus is righteous—100 percent righteous. In other words, Jesus, 100 percent of the time, did the right things that brought glory to the Father. Jesus did the work that the Father destined him to do.

"No one who abides in Him sins; no one who sins has seen Him or knows Him" (v. 6). The first statement in this verse is impossible: "No one who abides in Him sins." *Say what? No sin? That is unachievable.* In our own strength, that is a correct analysis. *In my conflict, I can't not sin.* Oh, yes, you can. However, if you believe you have to sin and mistreat people, then you will likely sin and mistreat people. But if you believe in the power of the Holy Spirit and the work of Jesus Christ, then it is possible to choose to not sin.

I am not saying we can assume we have not sinned and so do not need to humble ourselves and reflect on how we may have mistreated people. However, we should not give up fixing our eyes on Jesus and instead start practicing sin just because our excuse is we are fallen human beings.

Jesus is righteous; we practice righteousness. Practicing something does not automatically mean being perfect at it. Practicing is aiming for something. Practicing is deliberately doing our part to get better at something. Usually when we first start practicing something, we are not very good at it. However, the more we practice, the better we get. The apostle John talks about this idea. As you read through the following Scripture passage (perhaps out loud, repeating it three times), check out the appearance of the word *practice*.

No one who abides in Him sins; no one who sins has seen Him or knows Him. Little children, make sure no one deceives you; the one

who *practices* righteousness is righteous, just as He is righteous;
the one who *practices* sin is of the devil; for the devil has sinned
from the beginning. The Son of God appeared for this purpose,
to destroy the works of the devil. No one who is born of God
practices sin, because His seed abides in him; and he cannot sin,
because he is born of God. By this the children of God and the
children of the devil are obvious: anyone who does not *practice*
righteousness is not of God, nor the one who does not love his
brother. (vv. 6–10)

Let's break it down:

- Those who practice righteousness (doing the right thing
  that brings honor and glory to God) are righteous, just as
  Christ is righteous.
- Those who practice sin (disobedience to God and to his
  Word) are of the devil.

That initial analysis is fairly direct and transparent. Practice righteousness or practice sin. You are either of Christ or of the devil.
The passage does not stop at this point, though.

- No one born of God practices sin. The children of God
  practice righteousness.
- It is obvious that the children of the devil practice sin.

The kicker in John's argument is that if we do not love other people,
we are children of the devil. He is clearly pointing out that we need
to be reconcilers.

In short, Jesus is sinless, pure, holy, and righteous. And as children of God, so must we be.

To Be Sin on Our Behalf

He made Him who knew no sin *to be sin on our behalf*, so that
we might become the righteousness of God in Him. (2 Cor. 5:21)

188

The most concise Scripture reference I can find that describes this idea that Christ is "sin on our behalf" comes from the book of Philippians.

> Have this attitude in yourselves which was also in Christ Jesus, who, although He existed in the form of God, did not regard equality with God a thing to be grasped, but emptied Himself, taking the form of a bond-servant, and being made in the likeness of men. Being found in appearance as a man, He humbled Himself by becoming obedient to the point of death, even death on a cross. For this reason also, God highly exalted Him, and bestowed on Him the name which is above every name, so that at the name of Jesus every knee will bow, of those who are in heaven and on earth and under the earth, and that every tongue will confess that Jesus Christ is Lord, to the glory of God the Father. (Phil. 2:5–11)

Jesus clothed himself in humanity, humbled himself, and died so that he could reconcile us to himself. He took on sinful flesh. He is the atonement for our sin. The one who is 100 percent righteous died for those who are 100 percent unrighteous. Is this just or unjust? Well, the answer is both! From a human perspective it is unjust. From God's perspective it is just.

If we call ourselves Christ-followers, why is it we don't want to have the same attitude that Christ had, especially in our conflicts? We want to be 100 percent self-righteous. We want our reputation untarnished. We want to be vindicated. However, that is not the gospel on this side of heaven. Here on earth, our greatest point of injustice is our greatest opportunity to experience Christlikeness. Still don't believe me? Well, let's look back again at what Romans 5 has to say.

> For while we were still helpless, at the right time Christ died for the ungodly. For one will hardly die for a righteous man; though perhaps for the good man someone would dare even to die. But God demonstrates His own love toward us, in that while we were yet sinners, Christ died for us. Much more then, having now been justified by His blood, we shall be saved from the wrath of God

through Him. For if while we were enemies we were reconciled to God through the death of His Son, much more, having been reconciled, we shall be saved by His life. (vv. 6–10)

Look at what Jesus did for us while we were his enemies. Are we willing to have that same attitude for our enemies? We can't die for their salvation, because only Jesus can do that. However, we absolutely can have the same attitude of humility Christ demonstrated.

> Therefore if there is any encouragement in Christ, if there is any consolation of love, if there is any fellowship of the Spirit, if any affection and compassion, make my joy complete by being of the same mind, maintaining the same love, united in spirit, intent on one purpose. Do nothing from selfishness or empty conceit, but with humility of mind regard one another as more important than yourselves; do not merely look out for your own personal interests, but also for the interests of others. (Phil. 2:1–4)

Are you willing to die for others—for your enemies? Will you lay down your life for them? Will you lay down your rights? This requires having an attitude of humility. As believers, if we are going to have the same mind, maintain the same love, be united in spirit and intent on one purpose, and be reconcilers, we must have the same attitude as Christ, the true reconciler.

So That We Might Become the Righteousness of God in Him

> He made Him who knew no sin to be sin on our behalf, *so that we might become the righteousness of God in Him.* (2 Cor. 5:21)

Look at the outcome statement, "so that." This tiny phrase will change your life. Jesus died on our behalf *so that* we might become the righteousness of God in Jesus. You and I can become the righteousness of God. Wow! And this includes becoming the righteousness of God in our relationships. Can you believe it? What an honor.

But what does it actually mean to "become the righteousness of God"? Let's look at a couple of people the Bible labels as righteous.

> There was a man in the land of Uz whose name was Job; and that man was blameless, upright, fearing God and turning away from evil. (Job 1:1)

Now, Job lived way before Jesus. If Job can be described as blameless, upright, God-fearing, and a person who turned away from evil long before Jesus ever came to earth as a baby, then surely we can be described the same way, with resurrection power flowing through our lives and in our relationships. If you don't know the entire story of Job, I would encourage you to read it. Job suffered for the sake of righteousness. Personally, my suffering tends to be for the sake of unrighteousness, bad choices, or just simple selfishness.

For another example, let's look again at Luke's description of Zacharias and Elizabeth.

> In the days of Herod, king of Judea, there was a priest named Zacharias, of the division of Abijah; and he had a wife from the daughters of Aaron, and her name was Elizabeth. They were both righteous in the sight of God, walking blamelessly in all the commandments and requirements of the Lord. (Luke 1:5–6)

Wow! What a depiction of this married couple. Both were righteous and walked "blameless in all the commandments and requirements of the Lord." I marvel at this description. Oh, to follow the Lord's commands so well that I could be described as righteous and blameless.

But here is the interesting thing about all three of these individuals. They were righteous—but their lives were not easy. We can become the righteousness of God through faith in Jesus and still suffer. It happens. However, just because we are suffering doesn't mean we are supposed to do evil and curse God and others. The reason we reconcile with others is that, first, God tells us to do so in his Word and, second, because we have been reconciled.

Do you want to be in right standing with God? Do you desire to do the right things that honor and glorify him, especially in your conflict? Then let me encourage you—you can! You can because Jesus has made and is making you righteous.

To understand this in-process formation, let's go back to 1 John and look again at what it means to practice righteousness.

> No one who abides in Him sins; no one who sins has seen Him or knows Him. Little children, make sure no one deceives you; the one who *practices* righteousness is righteous, just as He is righteous; the one who *practices* sin is of the devil; for the devil has sinned from the beginning. The Son of God appeared for this purpose, to destroy the works of the devil. No one who is born of God *practices* sin, because His seed abides in him; and he cannot sin, because he is born of God. By this the children of God and the children of the devil are obvious: anyone who does not *practice* righteousness is not of God, nor the one who does not love his brother. (1 John 3:6–10)

Practicing righteousness means being kind to other people even when they are not kind to you (Eph. 4:32). We have such great opportunities to practice righteousness, especially when we experience injustice. Kindness is the key to reflecting the gospel. Kill the conflict with kindness. It is the most difficult thing to do. Meanness and rudeness are much easier. And yet, we are not only called to be kind in the presence of those who irritate or cause conflict with us but are called to be kind in their absence too. We are called to be kind in our thoughts. Kind in our attitudes. Kind in our interactions. We are to be kind even when the other person treats us with rudeness. Jesus showed this ultimate kindness on the cross when he cried out, "Father, forgive them; for they do not know what they are doing" (Luke 23:34).

Practicing righteousness means we become cling-ons. Yep, I said it. We must "cling to what is good" (Rom. 12:9). It is so easy to cling to what is wrong with someone else, but if we are going to be people who glorify God even when experiencing injustice, we must begin to cling to what God is doing and not to what other people are doing in their sin.

Practicing righteousness means living in restorative relationships: being kind, helping others, bearing each other's burdens (Gal. 6:2), and so on. Among humans, conflict will occur, so we must call on the righteousness we have in Jesus to restore these relationships. In our conflicts, we can't sow discord to reap peace; we must sow peace, and we will then reap peace.

Practicing righteousness is praying for those we are in conflict with—including praying for our enemy (James 5:16). I encourage you to sit down and pray for them. It really will make a tremendous difference in your attitude and response to conflict.

Now, you might be protesting, "What if they take advantage of me as I practice righteousness? It might become a totally unfair situation!" Let's see what Jesus has to say about that:

> Blessed are those who have been persecuted for the sake of righteousness, for theirs is the kingdom of heaven. Blessed are you when people insult you and persecute you, and falsely say all kinds of evil against you because of Me. Rejoice and be glad, for your reward in heaven is great; for in the same way they persecuted the prophets who were before you. (Matt. 5:10–12)

According to Jesus, you are blessed when you practice doing the things that honor and glorify God and your opponent persecutes you. This is probably not the answer you really wanted; however, Jesus set the greatest example of this for us all. Injustice will come, and you can still practice righteousness.

LIVING RECONCILED

Practical discoveries that will help you maintain reconciliation:

1. Conflict is inevitable, for we live in a fallen world.
2. Reconciliation is eventual. Seek to have an eternal perspective.

3. You have been given a pledge: you have the Holy Spirit to help you reconcile.

4. The gospel is real. Through the gospel message, you are emboldened to go crazy to glorify God.

5. Let Christ's love—not others—control you.

6. You have died, so you no longer live for yourself.

7. Consider your view; look at people the way God looks at them and not according to their fallenness.

8. As Christ is in us, we will see Christ in others too.

9. All believers have a ministry of reconciliation.

10. You have quit counting the faults of others. You have let go of the past.

11. God created you to be a reconciler, an ambassador for Christ.

12. Injustice will come, and you can still practice righteousness.

REVIEW AND RECAP

- Jesus relates to your weaknesses. He understands what you are going through. He understands every temptation, every struggle, every frustration, and every ounce of your sinfulness.

- We have such great opportunities to practice righteousness, especially when we experience injustice. Kindness is the key to reflecting the gospel. Kill the conflict with kindness.

- According to Jesus, you are blessed when you practice doing the things that honor and glorify God and your opponent persecutes you.

For God has not destined us for wrath, but for obtaining salvation through our Lord Jesus Christ, who died for us, so that whether we are awake or asleep, we will live together with Him. Therefore encourage one another and build up one another, just as you also are doing. But we request of you, brethren, that you appreciate those who diligently labor among you, and have charge over you in the Lord and give you instruction, and that you esteem them very highly in love because of their work. Live in peace with one another. We urge you, brethren, admonish the unruly, encourage the faint-hearted, help the weak, be patient with everyone. (1 Thess. 5:9–14)

TO MAKE YOU THINK

How can you encourage the person you are in conflict with despite your experience of injustice?

How can you build up those you are in conflict with despite your experience of injustice?

How can you live in peace with others despite injustice?

How can you be patient with others despite injustice?

WHY BE RECONCILED?

A Devotional Month

The ultimate key to being reconciled is to continue deliberately being in God's Word. To help you in this pursuit, this chapter is a thirty-one-day devotional. Take the time to go through each day of this guide. Study the Bible. Investigate! Immerse yourself in God's Word. Each day you will read a Scripture passage along with some key points and thoughts related to the passage and the topic of reconciliation and peacemaking. Then you will be challenged to apply God's Word to your current life situations.

I hope you enjoy this adventure of deeply studying God's Word and the path of peacemaking.

DAY 1

For if while we were enemies we were reconciled to God through the death of His Son, much more, having been reconciled, we shall be saved by His life.

Romans 5:10

Why Be Reconciled?

Reconcile because while you were an enemy, God reconciled with you.

Application

Who were we? We were enemies of God. That is a very strong statement. It wasn't just that we kind of dishonored God or somehow messed up a little; we were challengers, opponents, competitors against the Creator of the universe.

The Word of God is very clear: *while* we were enemies, Jesus died to reconcile fallen humanity to himself. Even as we fought against God, his Son was dying for us. That doesn't mean the entire world will embrace the reconciliation Jesus provides. In fact, God knows who his people are, and no one can come to reconciliation with the Father unless the Father draws them to himself.

At the same time we are drawn to the Father, we receive our ultimate challenge: to reconcile with others the way God reconciles. God didn't wait for us to build trust to reconcile. He didn't wait for us to become repentant to reconcile. The Father sent his Son to reconcile us to himself as a gift. Now, through faith we are reconciled, and so we must share that gift and reconcile with others.

In Conflict

- Are you willing to reconcile with the other person(s) you are in conflict with while they are still your enemy?
- Are you willing to offer a gift of reconciliation to the other person?
- How can you focus less on yourself during this conflict and allow the work of the cross to become more of your focus?

DAY 2

~~~~~

[Jesus prayed,] "I do not ask on behalf of these alone, but for those also who believe in Me through their word; that they may all be one; even as You, Father, are in Me and I in You, that they also may be in Us, so that the world may believe that You sent Me."

John 17:20–21

Why Be Reconciled?

Reconcile so that the world may believe that the Father sent Jesus.

Application

I would encourage you to read all of John 17. It is Jesus's final prayer before he is crucified. In this prayer, Jesus talks about unity and our mission here on earth as believers. Jesus repeats over and over that we are to be one with the Father and himself.

Read slowly and notice what Jesus is saying when he declares, "I do not ask on behalf of these alone." Jesus was praying for his disciples at the time, but he was also praying "for those who believe in Me through their word." Jesus is praying for you. Jesus is praying for me. *Why?* That we may believe in him through the message of the disciples.

He prays that we will be one. This is not just any type of unity he is seeking here. This unity is the same kind of unity that exists between the Father, Son, and Holy Spirit. Now that is amazing. Jesus prays that we will be unified with the Father and the Son *as they are unified.* Wow.

But take careful note of Jesus's primary reason for this type of unity: "So that the world may believe that You [the Father] sent Me" (v. 21).

In Conflict

- How might a unified, gospel-centered response bring one-ness to your conflict?
- How can you be an answer to Jesus's prayer even in the midst of your conflict?
- What specific actions can you take to bring about, at least for your part, this type of unity or peace?

DAY 3

For God did not send the Son into the world to judge the world, but that the world might be saved through Him.

John 3:17

Why Be Reconciled?

Reconcile because Jesus was sent into the world to save and not judge.

Application

John 3:16, the verse prior to today's verse, speaks of God's love for the entire world. It is clear that God the Father desires to see the world saved through his Son, Jesus Christ. In verse 18, Jesus says, "He who believes in Him is not judged," and he goes on to say, "He who does not believe has been judged already, because he has not believed in the name of the only begotten Son of God."

How does this verse apply to reconciliation? Let me explain.

In conflict, we can have a heart to judge or a heart to reconcile. A heart that desires reconciliation is of the gospel. It is so simple to fall into the trap of wanting your own justice, your own defense, your own vindication. However, God's heart is that the world be saved through Jesus. We need to have God's heart. For "the Lord is not slow about His promise, as some count slowness, but is patient toward you, not wishing for any to perish but for all to come to repentance" (2 Pet. 3:9). God's desire is that none should perish but all should come to repentance. If we are seeking after God's heart, we then will seek reconciliation and not judgment.

In Conflict

- Where is your heart set: judgment or reconciliation?
- Are you wanting the other person to come to repentance or to perish?
- Are you coming to repentance?
- What practical steps can you take to repent? What can you do to encourage repentance from the other person without judging them?

DAY 4

~~~~~

By this all men will know that you are My disciples, if you have love for one another.

<div align="right">John 13:35</div>

Why Be Reconciled?

Reconcile because the world is watching.

Application

The world is watching how the people of God interact. Are they seeing the gospel displayed before them? Or are they seeing selfishness and self-righteousness? As believers, we daily have an opportunity to display that we are God's disciples. This is not necessarily accomplished through silence or through volume. Rather, we can accomplish this display through a balance of speaking the truth in love to those around us.

Too often, when we think of love, we think of pretending conflict didn't happen or sweeping ugly behavior under the rug. It is not loving to let your friend, family member, or enemy walk off a cliff. Love gives them a warning. Love helps them see the danger ahead. It is equally not loving to micromanage, to try to mold another person into your image, or to control someone about preferences that will not harm them. Understanding the distinction between things that are dangerous and those that are preferences is a lifelong battle. However, true love has those kinds of critical conversations. These conversations should be filled with respect and always show tolerance for each other (Eph. 4:1–2).

Let it be stated of you that you are a person who displays the patience, self-control, and mercies of God that dwell inside of you through God's Word and are empowered by God's Holy Spirit.

In Conflict

- In how you are handling this conflict, would those involved who do not know God be attracted to the gospel?
- Are the areas you are fighting or in conflict about simply preferences, or are they truly things that are dangerous to you and/or the other person you are in conflict with?
- How might you show authentic love to the other person by laying down your rights for them?
- How might you demonstrate self-control by allowing the Holy Spirit to empower your differences?

DAY 5

~~~~~

Faithful are the wounds of a friend, but deceitful are the kisses of an enemy.

<div align="right">Proverbs 27:6</div>

Why Be Reconciled?

Reconcile because faithful are the wounds of a friend.

Application

Friendship can be tricky at times. Matters related to our hearts—relationships, friendships, love—are not to be taken lightly. This Scripture is about speaking the truth in love to your friends. It is not permission to wound people just because you can. We need each other in life. We also need to be honest with each other. An enemy will often tell us what we want to hear. A friend will often tell us what we need to hear.

If someone is being honest and transparent with you, then don't shoot the messenger. Their delivery may not be perfect. Their tone may not be to your preference. Their word choices might not be the best possible. The key is to sit back and listen. Take in the substance of their words. Learn from them and be teachable. They may be saying something to you that you can grow from—if you'll listen.

It can be incredibly difficult to be corrected by a friend. It also can be incredibly difficult to correct a friend. However, I have frequently seen silence toward bad behavior lead to the devastation of a marriage, a ministry, a family, a church. Please—I am begging you—humbly reflect and be humbly courageous. In both directions. Be willing to help others and be open to being helped by others.

In Conflict

- What is a friend trying to teach you right now?
- Are you listening?
- Have you spoken up about something you see in a friend that needs to be addressed in love?

DAY 6

Whether, then, you eat or drink or whatever you do, do all to the glory of God.

1 Corinthians 10:31

Why Be Reconciled?

Reconcile because reconciliation glorifies God.

Application

Glory is an interesting word. For many of us, or perhaps just for me, glory is not an everyday word. It can be defined as bringing attention to or giving full recognition to God. Before the fall, Adam and Eve fully gave glory to God. After the fall, humans can give God glory only through the redemptive work of Jesus Christ. If left to our own willpower, we will always bring attention to something other than God our Father.

Let's look at some contrasting thoughts about giving glory. Selfishness glorifies us. Selflessness glorifies God. Cursing, gossip, and slander do not glorify God. Honor, wholesome words, and praise do glorify God. Rage, fearmongering, and manipulation do not glorify God. Peace, love, and joy do glorify God.

Glorifying God, especially during conflict, is one of the greatest expressions of the gospel. It is a modest posture to bow low before God—giving him and only him our full attention. To glorify God, we must allow him to be honored and humbly embrace the work of the cross in our relationships.

In Conflict

- How can you bring attention to God in this conflict?
- How can you bring honor to the family of God during this conflict?
- What practical steps can you take to show humility?

DAY 7

~~~~~~

For He Himself is our peace, who made both groups into one and broke down the barrier of the dividing wall, by abolishing in His flesh the enmity, which is the Law of commandments contained in ordinances, so that in Himself He might make the two into one new man, thus establishing peace, and might reconcile them both in one body to God through the cross, by it having put to death the enmity.

Ephesians 2:14–16

Why Be Reconciled?

Reconcile because Jesus is our peace.

Application

Read that statement over and over: Jesus is our peace. Jesus, himself, is our peace. Now make it personal. Jesus, himself, is my peace. Jesus is your peace.

Jesus established peace by dying for the sin or enmity created by humans not following God's law. Jesus broke down the barrier between God and us. All people are able to be reconciled to God through Jesus. Sin was a wall that once divided humanity, separating us from God. Jesus kicked that wall down.

How does that apply to your current conflict? If Jesus broke down barriers that divide, shouldn't we imitate him and be willing to break down barriers that divide us from others? We are to imitate Christ (1 Cor. 11:1). Now, it is true that we don't die as a sin offering for the conflicts between us. However, Jesus died for our conflicts, and we embrace his death as the sin offering. In other words, we pick up our cross daily and follow Jesus. We embrace faith in Jesus. We are crucified with Christ (Gal. 2:20).

In Conflict

- What dividing wall is between you and the other person?
- From a practical standpoint, how can you show that Jesus broke down that barrier?
- What areas in this conflict need forgiveness?
- What areas in this conflict need repentance?

DAY 8

~~~

Therefore if there is any encouragement in Christ, if there is any consolation of love, if there is any fellowship of the Spirit, if any affection and compassion, make my joy complete by being of the same mind, maintaining the same love, united in spirit, intent on one purpose.

Philippians 2:1–2

Why Be Reconciled?

Reconcile because we are to maintain the same love.

Application

Are you encouraged in Jesus? Have you been consoled by his love? Do you have fellowship in the Spirit? Do you have the affection and compassion that come through Jesus? If you said yes to any of these, then I have to ask—what does your *sameness* look like?

We are to have the same mind. I don't know that this means we will see everything identically. It may mean we are to have the same mind of humility: gospel-focused, dying to self. This can be a challenge, especially when we are in conflict. However, through Jesus, all things are possible.

We are to maintain the same love. To *maintain* means this love may not come naturally or easily. People maintain their yards. It takes work—pruning, mowing, fertilizing, and watering. We need to be people who prune, mow, fertilize, and water our relationships, our love. Maintaining takes effort.

In Conflict

- What do you need to do to maintain the same love?
- How can you be united in spirit with the person you are in conflict with?
- How might you be intent on having one purpose with the person you are in conflict with?
- What might that purpose be?
- How is the gospel playing out in your conflicted relationship?

DAY 9

For one will hardly die for a righteous man; though perhaps for the good man someone would dare even to die. But God demonstrates His own love toward us, in that while we were yet sinners, Christ died for us.

Romans 5:7–8

Why Be Reconciled?

Reconcile because while we were still sinners Christ died for us.

Application

Very few will die to self for another person who is a sinner or completely in the wrong in a conflict. However, Christ died for us while we were still sinners. Think about that for a moment. In his eternal plan, God sent his one and only Son to die for sinners while we were still sinning.

What a clear demonstration of love. God is not willing to hold back his love simply because of our current state. That is powerful. Sure, we need to embrace the act of the gospel through faith and repentance. But even before we have taken those steps, God still loves us.

In conflict, demonstrating our love is one of the most difficult actions to take. It is challenging to show patience to others—especially when big emotions are involved. It is not easy to generously overflow kindness in our every interaction. Not being rude and not keeping a record of wrong are not natural. We may think we are doing well, but then the Holy Spirit often knocks on our door, and we realize we haven't succeeded as well as we thought.

In Conflict

- How are you demonstrating patience?
- How are you caring more for the other person than yourself?
- How are you not forcing yourself on others?
- How are you rejoicing in the truth?

DAY 10

~~~~~

If you address as Father the One who impartially judges according to each one's work, conduct yourselves in fear during the time of your stay on earth; knowing that you were not redeemed with perishable things like silver or gold from your futile way of life inherited from your forefathers, but with precious blood, as of a lamb unblemished and spotless, the blood of Christ. For He was foreknown before the foundation of the world, but has appeared in these last times for the sake of you who through Him are believers in God, who raised Him from the dead and gave Him glory, so that your faith and hope are in God.

1 Peter 1:17–21

Why Be Reconciled?

Reconcile because God will impartially judge.

Application

God is an impartial judge. Before you say, "Good, finally I'll see justice," let me remind you that God is an *impartial* judge. I don't

216

say that to scare you. However, remember that most people, before they go into a courtroom, have an inflated view of their case. They are typically 100 percent sure they are going to win, the judge will side with them, and victory is right around the corner. Which all may be true—but as God knows every motive, every thought, every word spoken in secret, your case may not be as guilt-free as you claim.

There is hope. You were redeemed by the blood of Jesus. *Redeemed* simply means purchased. Your sin was paid for. Your broken relationship was covered. Your contribution to the conflict tab has been picked up. Jesus shed his blood for your sin, their sin, and those other people's sins. God didn't redeem you with perishable goods. He redeemed you with the eternal body of his Son, Jesus.

In Conflict

- How have you become arrogant?
- Have you asked the impartial judge to search you?
- What has God revealed to you?
- Have you repented and accepted Jesus's work on the cross?

DAY 11

~~~~~~

Do nothing from selfishness or empty conceit, but with humility of mind regard one another as more important than
yourselves.

Philippians 2:3

Why Be Reconciled?

Reconcile because we are called to humility.

Application

Selfishness can be difficult to overcome during conflict. Selfishness
attacks our hearts and our minds. Think about the words we say
when we are being selfish: *I deserve this. I have given so much.
I am owed an apology. I am . . .* The word *I* is always the focus
of our attention. God's Word challenges us to do nothing from
selfishness. That nothing even includes conflict. Therefore, during
times of conflict, we need more selflessness, not selfishness.

Conceit that is empty is also very common, especially during
conflict. What is empty conceit? Empty conceit is a lot of talk
and little action. In conflict, it is easy to make idle threats either

verbally or mentally. Personally, in times of conflict I can begin to become conceited in my position and talk a big game. But when it comes down to it, it's just talk. We should have nothing to do with empty conceit before, during, or after conflict.

Humility of mind during conflict is very achievable when we add Jesus to its center. In fact, humility is the number one ingredient to reconciliation. You may not be reconciled even with humility, but you absolutely will not be reconciled without humility.

In Conflict

- How has selfishness driven your conflict?
- What empty or idle threats have you made during this conflict?
- What role is humility playing in this conflict?
- In what identifiable ways are you demonstrating that you see the other person as more important than yourself?

DAY 12

~~~~~

A new commandment I give to you, that you love one another, even as I have loved you, that you also love one another.

John 13:34

Why Be Reconciled?

Reconcile because we are commanded to love each other.

Application

"Love one another." How? "Even as I have loved you." So, how has Jesus loved you? I know I have hit this concept a lot in this book, but it bears repeating. Jesus loves you so much, he gave his life for you. This is how much we are to love those we are in conflict with—we must be willing to lay down our lives for them. Peter emphasized this point to the Christians he was encouraging: "Above all, keep fervent in your love for one another, because love covers a multitude of sins" (1 Pet. 4:8).

Fervent love for those we are in conflict with is not always easy to accomplish. But when we are patient and kind and sacrificial in response to conflict, those responses cover many wrongs.

In Conflict

- How has Jesus loved you?
- Are you loving the other person in your conflict in that same spirit?
- How are you being fervent in your love for them?
- Are you revealing their sin or allowing the blood of Christ to cover that sin?
- In your heart, are you revealing or continually replaying their sin, or are you praying for the blood of Jesus to cover it?

DAY 13

~~~~~~~

For it was the Father's good pleasure for all the fullness to
dwell in Him, and through Him to reconcile all things to
Himself, having made peace through the blood of His cross;
through Him, I say, whether things on earth or things in
heaven.

Colossians 1:19–20

Why Be Reconciled?

Reconcile because Christ's blood brings peace.

Application

Have you ever sat down and thought about the Father's good pleasure? This verse points out two things that please God. First, God
is pleased for the fullness of God and the fullness of humankind to
dwell in Jesus Christ. Second, it pleases God for Jesus to reconcile
all things to the Father.

This amazing act of the reconciliation of all things occurred
through the shedding of Jesus's blood. The blood of Jesus is what
creates peace with God the Father. This peace is what the world is

looking for—what all individuals seek in their hearts and in their daily living. The blood of Jesus is reconciling and has reconciled all believers to the Father. It is the payment for our sin.

However, in times of conflict, I often want something other than the blood of Christ to bring peace. I want the other person to truly repent. I want the other person to feel sorrow. I want the other person to never do whatever they did again. Let me be very clear: it is nice when the other person authentically repents, feels sorrow for their sin, and never does an offensive action again. However, this is not peace. Peace is not dependent on another person. Peace only comes through the payment for sin, and that was made through the blood of Jesus Christ. Peace hinges on Jesus Christ and the sacrifice he made on the cross.

In Conflict

- What are some practical things I can do to realize that the fullness dwells in Jesus?
- How does that fullness give me hope?
- How am I trying to get fullness from something or someone else?
- How am I trying to reconcile through human efforts instead of through Christ?
- How am I accepting the work on the cross to bring peace to my current situation?
- How can I view this conflict through the work on the cross?

DAY 14

~~~~~~~~

Brethren, even if anyone is caught in any trespass, you who are spiritual, restore such a one in a spirit of gentleness; each one looking to yourself, so that you too will not be tempted.

<div align="right">Galatians 6:1</div>

Why Be Reconciled?

Reconcile because gentle restoration is God's plan.

Application

Have you been caught in a trespass? Are you on someone else's land where you should not be? Has someone trespassed on you? In conflict, it is very easy to trespass and go over the property line. To find yourself in the middle of someone else's field, trampling on their emotions and story. Or to simply sin against someone else.

A Christ-follower calls trespassers out and off of the land that does not belong to them. We have been transferred into God's kingdom, and anytime we find ourselves living like we are in the enemy's kingdom, we are on land we should not be on. Acts of our flesh—sin—make us trespassers. Conflict can bring out the worst in us and draw us into being trespassers.

Now, a Christ-follower is to lead a trespasser off the land—but they are to do so gently. Gentle restoration! Why? Gentleness requires humility. And having a humble view of oneself is important; we need to recognize we all can trespass at times. Gentleness allows us to recognize that we need others to help us see our own blind spots—the areas of sin or weakness we cannot see or identify for ourselves.

In Conflict

- How can you gently restore someone you are in conflict with?
- Have you reflected inwardly to see how you might be tempted to trespass in the same way?
- Are you willing to ask the other person to share with you your own blind spots?
- How have you trespassed against the other person?

DAY 15

Have this attitude in yourselves which was also in Christ Jesus.

Philippians 2:5

Why Be Reconciled?

Reconcile because reconciliation is Jesus's attitude.

Application

What is your attitude like? How has your attitude gotten better since your conflict first began? How has it gotten worse? Our attitude plays an important role in handling conflict. If we feel hopeless, we will approach the conflict without hope. If we view the conflict as an opportunity to glorify God, we will be more than likely to approach it that way.

The rest of the Philippians 2 passage describes the attitude Christ Jesus had,

> who, although He existed in the form of God, did not regard equality with God a thing to be grasped, but emptied Himself, taking the form of a bond-servant, and being made in the likeness of

men. Being found in appearance as a man, He humbled Himself by becoming obedient to the point of death, even death on a cross. (vv. 6–8)

In conflict, we can either empty ourselves or, through pride, build ourselves up. If we empty ourselves, we let go of our agenda, our opinions, and our need for self-justification and leave that space open for God's agenda, opinion, and justification. It is so easy to think more highly of our response to conflict than we really should. In fact, we will often go around and ask others for their opinions on how we're responding, hoping they agree with us.

The reality is we are to pick up our crosses and follow Jesus. We absolutely need to do this when it comes to our actions, our attitudes, our conversations, and our side conversations.

In Conflict

- What is your attitude like in this conflict? Are you picking up your cross or building yourself up?
- In this conflict, how are you emptying yourself?
- How might you die to yourself in this conflict?
- How might you have the attitude of Christ?

DAY 16

~~~~~~~~

> Be imitators of me, just as I also am of Christ.
>
> 1 Corinthians 11:1

Why Be Reconciled?

Reconcile because we are to imitate Christ even in our conflicts.

Application

When we think of the word *imitation*, we often associate it with *fake*—something that looks real but isn't. For example, if I say imitation crab, you think of crab that looks like crab but really isn't crab. That is not what imitation is referring to in this passage. Let me put in front of you the Greek word for *imitators*:

> **3401. μιμέομαι miméomai**; contracted *mimoúmai*, fut. *mimḗsomai*, mid. deponent from *mímos* (n.f.), an imitator. To mimic, but in a good sense, to imitate, follow as an example, with the acc. (2 Thess. 3:7, 9; Heb. 13:7; 3 John 1:11).[1]

Imitators are followers, or those who mimic or copy the example of another person—in other words, *disciples*. Think of how Christ responded to conflict. Sometimes he got angry. Sometimes he corrected others. Sometimes he gave grace. Sometimes he was bold. Sometimes he was gentle. But no matter what his response, he never sinned. The problem is, we like to compare our responses to Christ's responses to make excuses for our sinful behavior when the reality is Jesus never sinned. It's okay to be bold. It's okay to correct, rebuke, and train in righteousness. It's also okay to be teachable and have an attitude of humility. Imitate Christ in conflict—that includes not sinning in your response.

In Conflict

- How are you imitating Christ?
- How can you give grace like Christ gives grace?
- How can you be bold like Christ is bold?

DAY 17

The one who says, "I have come to know Him," and does not keep His commandments, is a liar, and the truth is not in him; but whoever keeps His word, in him the love of God has truly been perfected. By this we know that we are in Him: the one who says he abides in Him ought himself to walk in the same manner as He walked.

1 John 2:4–6

Why Be Reconciled?

Reconcile because we are to walk in the same manner as Jesus walked.

Application

To say, "I have come to know Christ" is a bold statement. What is even bolder is to declare we know Christ and yet not keep his commandments. In fact, that makes us liars. Especially when we couple these verses with this statement later in 1 John:

If someone says, "I love God," and hates his brother, he is a liar; for the one who does not love his brother whom he has seen, cannot love God whom he has not seen. (4:20)

Jesus never walked in hate. He continually walked in love. So if we are bold enough to declare we know Christ, then we must be bold in walking in love. Love is not an excuse for injustice. True love recognizes an injustice and holds harder to Jesus than to the injustice. It doesn't mean there isn't a need for accountability. The Bible even says that ultimately God is the true source of accountability (Rom. 12:19). However, for our purposes, love doesn't keep a record of wrong. Love does not hate.

In Conflict

- How are you walking like Jesus in your present conflict?
- Are you holding others to God's accountability rather than your accountability?
- Are you lying to yourself?
- How is God's Word abiding in you?

DAY 18

~~~~~~~~

So, as those who have been chosen of God, holy and beloved, put on a heart of compassion, kindness, humility, gentleness and patience; bearing with one another, and forgiving each other, whoever has a complaint against anyone; just as the Lord forgave you, so also should you.

Colossians 3:12–13

Why Be Reconciled?

Reconcile because you are chosen of God.

Application

God chose you. You are beloved and pronounced holy because of him. That is a lot to process. Do not overlook the significance of being chosen of God. He desires that you be on his team, of his kingdom, one of his children. You are a part of God's family.

In God's family, we are to put on a heart of compassion, kindness, humility, gentleness, and patience. This getting dressed as God would have us be dressed applies even to our conflicts. Conflicts would change so much if we simply did what the Scriptures say to do. We can have a variety of complaints against each other. The key is whether or not we are forgiving the way that Jesus forgave us.

Bearing up—tolerating, putting up with—the person you are in conflict with is not easy. It takes an act of surrendering to the Holy Spirit who dwells in you. But remember, God chose you—he has not called you in his Word to something he has not empowered and equipped you to do.

In Conflict

- How does knowing you are carrying the family (God's family) name cause you to respond differently to others?
- What would compassion look like in your present conflict?
- Creatively, how might you be kind to the other person?

DAY 19

Let all bitterness and wrath and anger and clamor and slander be put away from you, along with all malice. Be kind to one another, tender-hearted, forgiving each other, just as God in Christ also has forgiven you.

Ephesians 4:31–32

Why Be Reconciled?

Reconcile because we let go of bitterness.

Application

Bitterness will kill you. Wrath will depress you. Anger will annoy you. Clamor will inflame you. Slander will indict you. Let go of all of it. Put it away at the foot of the cross. Holding on to these will not do you any good. However, after emptying yourself, don't leave an empty hole. Fill the hole with godly attributes.

Kindness and tenderheartedness are powerful during conflict. With kindness, you can serve the other person. With tenderheartedness, you can draw them back into relationship. Ask yourself: *In the view of eternity, how important is this conflict?*

God has forgiven you through Jesus Christ by throwing your sin into the depths of the sea. He has forgiven you by putting all your sin behind his back and under his feet. God doesn't focus on your sin any longer—he chooses not to remember it. He doesn't define you by your sin.

In Conflict

- What bitterness do you need to get rid of?
- How has your anger gotten out of control?
- What would tenderheartedness look like in this conflict?
- How can you throw this conflict into the depths of the sea?
- What is a new way you can define the other person besides through the conflict?

DAY 20

~~~~~~~~

Be on your guard! If your brother sins, rebuke him; and if he repents, forgive him. And if he sins against you seven times a day,
and returns to you seven times, saying, "I repent," forgive him.

<div align="right">Luke 17:3–4</div>

Why Be Reconciled?

Reconcile because repentance leads to forgiveness.

Application

Some have read this set of Bible verses believing they mean that
if the other person in a conflict does not repent, then they do not
have to forgive that person. In fact, I've had several well-meaning
Christians say this directly to me. However, that is not what Jesus
is teaching us here. He is not teaching us that we get to remain
bitter, angry, and mad because someone else has not repented.
We cannot withhold forgiveness because of someone else's lack
of repentance.

Jesus is teaching us more about the frequency of forgiveness
than the conditions of forgiveness. I squarely believe forgiveness

is based more on Jesus—his death and resurrection—and less on our ability to feel forgiveness.

A restored relationship requires repentance. If someone gives you the gift of forgiveness based on Jesus, and you reject that gift by not repenting, that is your choice. If you forgive someone else and they reject your gift, you have still done as the Lord asks of you. That is why Romans clearly states, "as far as it depends on you, live at peace with everyone" (12:18). We can have a heart of forgiveness even before repentance occurs.

In Conflict

- How are you doing in talking to the other person about their sin?
- Are your conversations productive or destructive?
- How could you make your conversations more productive?
- How are you doing at forgiving the other person—even if they repeat their sin or refuse to repent?

DAY 21

~~~~~

Bless those who persecute you; bless and do not curse. Rejoice with those who rejoice, and weep with those who weep. Be of the same mind toward one another; do not be haughty in mind, but associate with the lowly. Do not be wise in your own estimation. Never pay back evil for evil to anyone. Respect what is right in the sight of all men. If possible, so far as it depends on you, be at peace with all men. Never take your own revenge, beloved, but leave room for the wrath of God, for it is written, "Vengeance is Mine, I will repay," says the Lord. But if your enemy is hungry, feed him, and if he is thirsty, give him a drink; for in so doing you will heap burning coals on his head. Do not be overcome by evil, but overcome evil with good.

Romans 12:14–21

Why Be Reconciled?

Reconcile because we are to bless those who persecute us.

Application

Blessing your persecutor is probably the hardest action to take in the middle of conflict. The second most difficult action is to not

238

curse them in your thinking or in your heart. Third most difficult is to overcome evil with good. However, when you trust God as the just Judge, all of this becomes much easier. When you rely on the power of the Holy Spirit, it becomes even easier still. There is so much we can learn from these verses. Take your time and reflect on them—always keeping in perspective that when we trust the power, love, and justice that are beyond us, we are more than conquerors of our challenges.

In Conflict

- How can you bless the person you are in conflict with?
- How can you overcome evil with good?
- How might you try to live at peace with them?
- Have you done your part to live at peace with them?
- Are you leaning on the justice of God and the power of the Holy Spirit?

DAY 22

~~~~~

To sum up, all of you be harmonious, sympathetic, brotherly, kindhearted, and humble in spirit; not returning evil for evil or insult for insult, but giving a blessing instead; for you were called for the very purpose that you might inherit a blessing.

1 Peter 3:8–9

Why Be Reconciled?

Reconcile because harmonious living is God's standard.

Application

Yes, I know this Bible verse feels a lot like yesterday's verse. I am intentionally repeating myself so that you will know the same concept from two different authors. In this passage, Peter is summing up his thoughts. We are to be harmonious. We are to live in unity of mind. We are to interact with kindheartedness and humility.

Do not return evil for evil. Do not return insult for insult. It's very easy in conflict to fail and do the opposite. The person I'm in conflict with said this, so I did that in retaliation. They emailed, so I posted. They criticized me, so I criticized them.

Stop! We are to bless, not curse. That is why we were called. This is why we were created: for the purpose of being a blessing. That is amazing to think about. You were called for the purpose of blessing others. I love how *The Message* presents this passage:

> Summing up: Be agreeable, be sympathetic, be loving, be compassionate, be humble. That goes for all of you, no exceptions. No retaliation. No sharp-tongued sarcasm. Instead, bless—that's your job, to bless. You'll be a blessing and also get a blessing. (1 Pet. 3:8–9)

In Conflict

- How can you be agreeable in this conflict?
- How can you be sympathetic?
- How can you practically give a blessing?

DAY 23

~~~~~~

Do not say, "I will repay evil"; Wait for the Lord, and He will save you.

<div align="right">Proverbs 20:22</div>

Why Be Reconciled?

Reconcile because we are waiting for the Lord.

Application

Waiting on the Lord can be exceptionally difficult. At times, he seems to move very slowly. I can remember in junior high mistreating someone who'd mistreated me and saying, "Payback!" God's Word says no to paybacks.

God is the protector of your reputation—not you. He will save your reputation. This is for his name's sake. He is the one who will rescue you. He is the one who repairs and restores you. It may take time. It may be in eternity, but you have no business repaying evil with more evil.

I would have despaired unless I had believed that I would
  see the goodness of the LORD
In the land of the living.
Wait for the LORD;
Be strong and let your heart take courage;
Yes, wait for the LORD. (Ps. 27:13–14)

In Conflict

- In your conflict, are there areas in which you need to wait on the Lord?
- What are those areas? Be specific.
- How have you tried to take the law into your own hands?
- How can you continue to be strong in the law of the Lord?
- How can you continue to be courageous?

DAY 24

~~~~~

This you know, my beloved brethren. But everyone must be quick to hear, slow to speak and slow to anger; for the anger of man does not achieve the righteousness of God.

James 1:19–20

Why Be Reconciled?

Reconcile because your anger does not achieve God's righteousness.

Application

Quick, be a listener! Listen in the middle of conflict? That is a high goal to have. When we are in conflict, we often talk way more than we listen. The number one thing that can save us a lot of grief in conflict is to shut our mouths and listen. I wish I could always apply this truth in all my relationships, especially my home relationships. However, let's be clear. This is not just about not talking; this is about active listening. This is where you are truly trying to hear what the other person has to say. You value what they say, so you listen.

If you are like me, your jaws can get to flapping and saying things that should not be said. The key is to truly stop and listen to their words. And then, before you talk, think about what you are going to say. What words are you going to use to release God's grace into the moment?

Be slow to anger. Anger is interesting: some people are explosive while others are internal stewers. Your fleshly anger will not achieve God's righteousness. We need to watch, control, and surrender our anger to God. Our anger needs to be only righteous anger that is expressed through the hope of the gospel.

In Conflict

- How can you better actively listen in your present conflict?
- What words can you use to express God's love and grace?
- How might you express your anger through the gospel?

DAY 25

A hot-tempered man stirs up strife, but the slow to anger calms a dispute.

Proverbs 15:18

Why Be Reconciled?

Reconcile because it will calm a dispute.

Application

Reconciliation with others always starts with reconciling with God. Every sin we commit against each other is really a sin against God. When we slow down our anger, control our tongues, and reconcile with God, it will calm the dispute. We must learn to express our disappointment and frustration to him first. Only then will we begin to see a vast difference in our conflicts.

Anger can get out of control. Typically, this occurs because our tongues get out of control. It always amazes me how fast anger can move throughout my entire being. A constant prayer, a surrendered prayer, is one that says, "God, let me be a person who calms a dispute. Help me to bridle or control my tongue."

James has a lot to say about our tongues and our ability to calm a dispute.

> If anyone thinks himself to be religious, and yet does not bridle his tongue but deceives his own heart, this man's religion is worthless. (James 1:26)

> But no one can tame the tongue; it is a restless evil and full of deadly poison. With it we bless our Lord and Father, and with it we curse men, who have been made in the likeness of God. (3:8–9)

In Conflict

- How are you calming the dispute?
- How are you controlling your tongue?
- Are there things you said that you need to repent of?
- How can you speak well of the other person—to yourself, to them, to others?
- How can you share your love toward them?

DAY 26

~~~~~~~~~

A man's discretion makes him slow to anger, and it is his glory to overlook a transgression.

<div align="right">Proverbs 19:11</div>

Why Be Reconciled?

Reconcile vertically because it is to your glory to overlook a sin.

Application

Vertical reconciliation is taking an injustice toward you and handing it over to God by laying it down at the cross. This often happens through prayer. Vertical reconciliation is intentional. It is purposeful. It is dramatically different than just sweeping an injustice under the rug.

This verse always intrigues me. I think it is because it says the person who overlooks transgressions receives glory, yet I have been taught that all glory should go to God. I am not 100 percent sure what this means or how to process it. All I know is God loves it when we don't pick at every injustice or insist that we must always be treated perfectly all of the time.

Day 26

The great part about vertical reconciliation—reconciliation in which you take an injustice you experienced or caused to the Lord, despite how the other person responds—is that nobody can steal that type of reconciliation from you.

Vertical reconciliation is completely based on Jesus and his work on the cross. It is not based on anything else or anyone else. It is always available. It is always present. Jesus can make you complete no matter what anyone else says or does.

In Conflict

- How can you embrace reconciliation with God despite a lack of reconciliation with another person?
- What can you tangibly do to embrace the reconciliation Jesus brings to the cross even when the other person does not want to embrace that type of reconciliation?

DAY 27

~~~~~~

But Joseph said to them, "Do not be afraid, for am I in God's place?"

<div align="right">Genesis 50:19</div>

Why Be Reconciled?

Reconcile because we are not in the place of God.

Application

I would love to teach you all of Joseph's testimony. His family mistreated him. His employer falsely accused him. His friends forgot him. He is a great example of the gospel foreshadowing that occurs throughout the Old Testament. Go read Joseph's story in Genesis 37 to 50. Especially focus on Genesis 45—this is the point in the story when he encounters his brothers again and has to decide how to respond to them.

At the end of the story, his brothers are afraid that Joseph may still have a grudge—and at this point, Joseph holds a lot of power. The brothers tell Joseph a lie. Joseph responds by saying, "Do not be afraid." I do not know about you, but if I experienced decades of injustices because of my brothers' actions, I am not sure my response would be, "Do not be afraid." But he doesn't even stop there. He says, "Am I in God's place?" Wow! That is powerful. Joseph had all the power of Egypt—and yet he did not equate himself to God.

In conflict, it is incredibly easy to think of ourselves as being in God's position. We often see ourselves as judge, jury, and executioner. Let your heart and actions proclaim that in your conflict you do not think you're in the place of God. Joseph's story finishes with this statement: "And he comforted his brothers" (50:21 AMP).

In Conflict

- How have you judged the other person and, in a way, played God?
- Have you wanted the other person to experience fear?
- How have you used your anger to cause fear in the other person?
- How might you comfort those you are in conflict with?

DAY 28

~~~~~~

Therefore I want the men in every place to pray, lifting up holy hands, without wrath and dissension.

<div align="right">1 Timothy 2:8</div>

Why Be Reconciled?

Reconcile because we are challenged to worship without dissension.

Application

Prayer is powerful. Lifting up our hands to the Lord is an honor. He simply asks us in his Word to do so without wrath and dissension. Let me share this verse in a couple of different translations.

> I desire then that in every place the men should pray, lifting holy hands without anger or quarreling. (v. 8 ESV)

> Since prayer is at the bottom of all this, what I want mostly is for men to pray—not shaking angry fists at enemies but raising holy hands to God. (v. 8 Message)

Our enemy, or the person we are in conflict with, may make us incredibly angry. We might want to shake our fists at them. Instead, when we trust God, we can open our hands and exalt and praise our God—the Creator of our hands. Our hands were made for praise. Our hands were made to glorify God, not to threaten our fellow human beings.

In Conflict

- How can you repurpose your hands for God's glory?
- Have you threatened others outwardly?
- Have you threatened others internally?
- How might you change your threats into praise?
- What would it look like to lift up your holy hands in worship to God?

DAY 29

As a result, we are no longer to be children, tossed here and there by waves and carried about by every wind of doctrine, by the trickery of men, by craftiness in deceitful scheming; but speaking the truth in love, we are to grow up in all aspects into Him who is the head, even Christ, from whom the whole body, being fitted and held together by what every joint supplies, according to the proper working of each individual part, causes the growth of the body for the building up of itself in love.

Ephesians 4:14–16

Why Be Reconciled?

Reconcile because we are to no longer be like children.

Application

Is your conflict tossing you around? Do you feel like a storm has overtaken your life? We are to have childlike faith but mature responses to conflict. What is a mature response? We are to speak the truth in love to each other. In this passage, Paul is speaking specifically about our doctrine. If this passage is just about doctrine, how much more should we speak the truth in love in our daily lives? The doctrines we live by should be at the root of our daily behavior. They are the core of who we are. If we are to speak truth in love in those deepest areas of our beliefs, then isn't it safe to say that, as our doctrine flows out of us, we should speak truth in love in the simpler things of life too?

We will grow up into Christ when we encounter God's Word in this way. Think through this idea. We are the body of Christ. We are his hands, his feet, his legs, his neck, and so much more. When we work in harmony with the head, we do not try to go our own way. We allow the head to direct us, and he causes us to grow.

In Conflict

- Practically, how are you speaking truth in love into your conflict?
- Is the truth you are speaking your preference, or is it actually God's truth from his Word?
- How are you demonstrating God's mature patience in this conflict?

DAY 30

~~~~~

He who conceals his transgressions will not prosper, but he who confesses and forsakes them will find compassion.

Proverbs 28:13

Why Be Reconciled?

Reconcile because it provides an avenue to confess and forsake our sin and find compassion from God.

Application

Confess and forsake your sin. God is a compassionate God. He is slow to anger and abounding in lovingkindness. The problem is, when we confess to others, they will often use that information against us. They will bring up those sins over and over again. And yet, even with the risk of the misuse of our confession, it is worth finding compassion.

Confessing is telling God and others you were wrong. It is so important to humbly reflect on God's Word and allow his Holy Spirit to convict you so that you can make a thorough confession.

Forsaking is turning from our sin. This is where we commit not to do that sin again. We also commit to walk in behavior and transformation that bring glory to God. So many people try to stop doing a specific sin but never start anything new to transform their lives. And so they only find themselves back in the same spot they were again and again.

In Conflict

- What do you need to confess?
- How will you practically forsake what you confessed?
- How can you show God is working in your life by walking in newness of life?
- How will you show that newness of life to others?

DAY 31

~~~~

Therefore if you are presenting your offering at the altar, and there remember that your brother has something against you, leave your offering there before the altar and go; first be reconciled to your brother, and then come and present your offering.

Matthew 5:23–24

Why Be Reconciled?

Reconcile because Jesus says reconciling comes above even worship.

Application

A lack of reconciliation will interrupt your worship, both your corporate worship at church and your private worship through-out the week. Have you ever said, "If they have a problem with me, then they need to come and talk to me"? I have. Yet in this verse, Jesus says the opposite. I wonder if, during our times at the altar or other times of interacting with God, the Holy Spirit isn't quietly prompting us, saying, *Make your relationship right with the other person.*

I love how this idea is paraphrased in *The Message*:

This is how I want you to conduct yourself in these matters. If you enter your place of worship and, about to make an offering, you suddenly remember a grudge a friend has against you, abandon your offering, leave immediately, go to this friend and make things right. Then and only then, come back and work things out with God. (Matt. 5:23–24)

In Conflict

- Have you remembered an offense someone has toward you? Write it down. Think it through.
- Have you done all that you can to make peace with them (Rom. 12:18)?
- Write out the practical steps you will take to reconcile with them. Hint: the previous twelve chapters have some great ideas on where to start this process!

ACKNOWLEDGMENTS

Thank you to my father, my dad, who taught me a strong work ethic. He raised me to live by my principles and showed me what it is to work hard. To my mom, who showed me consistency. She also showed me how to help others and taught me hospitality. To my stepdad, who taught me to go the extra mile, to plan for the future, and how to be a family. To my stepmom, who showed me the value of justice and fairness. To my wife and amazing kids. To the churches that God has entrusted me to pastor, lead, and direct over the past twenty-plus years.

NOTES

Chapter 2 Be Brave

1. Walter Mote, "My Hope Is Built on Nothing Less," 1834, public domain, https://hymnary.org/text/my_hope_is_built_on_nothing_less.

2. Warren Baker and Eugene E. Carpenter, *The Complete Word Study Dictionary: Old Testament* (Chattanooga, TN: AMG Publishers, 2003), 1152.

3. Spiros Zodhiates, ed., *The Complete Word Study Dictionary: New Testament* (Chattanooga, TN: AMG Publishers, 2000), 3772.

Chapter 4 Go Crazy for God's Glory

1. Spiros Zodhiates, ed., *The Complete Word Study Dictionary: New Testament* (Chattanooga, TN: AMG Publishers, 2000), 2476.

Chapter 5 Courageous Attitude 1

1. Spiros Zodhiates, ed., *The Complete Word Study Dictionary: New Testament*, s.v. "grace" (Chattanooga, TN: AMG Publishers, 2000), 5485.

Chapter 10 Courageous Attitude 6

1. Martin Luther King Jr., "Loving Your Enemies," sermon delivered at the Dexter Avenue Baptist Church, Montgomery, Alabama, December 25, 1957.

Chapter 11 Courageous Attitude 7

1. *Merriam-Webster's Collegiate Dictionary*, s.v. "ambassador," Merriam-Webster, accessed March 10, 2021, https://unabridged.merriam-webster.com/collegiate/ambassador.

2. Spiros Zodhiates, ed., *The Complete Word Study Dictionary: New Testament*, s.v. "aphíēmi" (Chattanooga, TN: AMG Publishers, 2000).

3. Zodhiates, *Complete Word Study Dictionary*, s.v. "charízomai."

4. Zodhiates, *Complete Word Study Dictionary*, s.v. "katallássō."

Why Be Reconciled? Day 16

1. Spiros Zodhiates, ed., *The Complete Word Study Dictionary: New Testament*, s.v. "miméomai" (Chattanooga, TN: AMG Publishers, 2000).

P. Brian Noble is an everyday guy who loves Jesus and cares deeply about people's relationships. He has been married to his best friend, Tanya, for over twenty years; they have four children and currently reside in eastern Washington. He is the CEO of Peacemaker Ministries and has been an ordained minister for over twenty years.

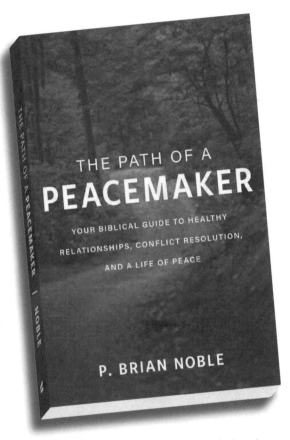

PEACEMAKER®
— ministries —

Peacemaker Ministries is a nonprofit, nondenominational ministry whose mission is to equip and assist Christians and their churches to respond to conflict biblically. We want to partner with people in conflict and help them navigate their conflict and heal their relationships.

Head to **www.peacemakerministries.org** to learn more.

 Peacemaker

 PMMinistries

 PeacemakerMinistries

LOOKING FOR MORE PEACEMAKING CONTENT?

Read the Peacemaker
Ministries Devotionals at
blog.peacemakerministries.org.